SpringerBriefs in Law

More information about this series at http://www.springer.com/series/10164

Tibor Tajti · Peter Iglikowski

A Cross Border Study of Freezing Orders and Provisional Measures

Does Mareva Rule the Waves?

Springer

Tibor Tajti
Department of Legal Studies
Central European University
Budapest, Hungary

Peter Iglikowski
Paris Descartes University
Paris, France

ISSN 2192-855X ISSN 2192-8568 (electronic)
SpringerBriefs in Law
ISBN 978-3-319-94348-0 ISBN 978-3-319-94349-7 (eBook)
https://doi.org/10.1007/978-3-319-94349-7

Library of Congress Control Number: 2018945900

Printed on acid-free paper

This Springer imprint is published by the registered company Springer International Publishing AG part of Springer Nature
The registered company address is: Gewerbestrasse 11, 6330 Cham, Switzerland

[Unlike in the bygone age of slow-moving capital and comparatively immobile wealth, today] increasingly sophisticated foreign-haven judgment proofing strategies, coupled with technology that permits the nearly instantaneous transfer of assets abroad, suggests that defendants may succeed in avoiding meritorious claims in ways unimaginable before the merger of law and equity.[1]

[1]From the concurring and dissenting opinion in *Grupo Mexicano de DeSarrollo, S.A. v. Alliance Bond Fund, Inc.* 527 U.S. 308 (1999). [Hereinafter: *Grupo Mexicano*].

Preface

The idea of a cross-border study of arrest measures originated from a public lecture delivered in April 2013 at CEU in Budapest comparing the English Mareva Injunction (Freezing Order) with the French Civil Law Conservative Arrest (Saisie Conservatoire). After the lecture, Professor Tajti invited his English colleague to write an article on the subject for publication. It occurred to both authors in the course of editing the text that there was surprisingly little literature devoted to comparative studies of provisional measures involving the arrest of assets. Consequently, the scope of the paper was considerably extended resulting in the present work.

The authors decided that the inclusion of another major jurisdiction outside of Europe (the USA) would be very beneficial to the examination of the issues discussed. And then, the further decision was taken to incorporate a review of the existing law of an emergent former Soviet Bloc state in Central Europe to highlight some of the shortcomings of legal systems which had not yet developed their law in this field. The final work is a comprehensive survey of the provisional measures of France and the UK, including, by way of contrast, a presentation of the law of the USA representing a very developed jurisdiction in comparison with the less developed state of the law of Hungary, a traditional legal system of Central Europe.

In the quest for a model for interim relief, the English Mareva Injunction, subsequently renamed as the 'Freezing Order', is taken as the benchmark to which each of the targeted systems herein are primarily compared. This is because international scholarship, as well as the US Supreme Court, positions the Mareva Injunction as the most efficient and most far-reaching provisional remedy known today deserving its label of the '*nuclear weapon of the law*'.

Besides giving a comparison of English and US law on provisional measures, this monograph uniquely analyses not only the distinguishing features of the widely used French *Saisie Conservatoire* but also the so far neglected Hungarian law; each of them representing a distinct approach. While English law relies on injunctions as in personam relief, French law achieves comparable results by employing the *in rem Saisie Conservatoire*. As opposed to the latter solutions, US law combines the two yet affords more weight to remedies within *rem effects*. Hungarian law represents out of the four the only system that has survived without *ex parte provisional* measures so far.

Yet, it is not only the scarcity of comparative law scholarship in this area that makes the topic of provisional measures of heightened importance. The increased speed with which commerce is unfolding in the twenty-first century inevitably makes the value of provisional measures of greater significance, because they are the effective tools in the hands of courts which can redress abuses and inequalities among the parties. The speed with which things change obviously is and will continue to be dictated by the ever-faster advancing technologies. So, as the concurring and dissenting Justices of the US Supreme Court expressed in the famous Grupo Mexicano case in 1999, the '*age of slow-moving capital and comparatively immobile wealth*' is bygone and the twenty-first century requires a fresh look at the law of provisional measures.

It should not come as a surprise consequently that the European Union found it important to introduce its own version of provisional measures, the European Account Preservation Order (EAPO), or that the Uniform Law Commission of the USA launched its Uniform Asset-Protection Orders Act not long ago in 2012. Consequently, it was important to reflect on these developments in the book as well.

It is by no means a coincidence that text which follows is the collaboration of an academic and a practising lawyer. Leaving aside its obvious academic interest, the subject is of course of immense practical importance. Every legal advisor knows that obtaining a favourable judgment in a legal action is of little benefit to a client if it cannot be successfully enforced against its debtor. The English author has been practising in the arena of international litigation for over thirty years and has considerable experience of the problems encountered in attempting to enforce arbitration awards or judgments. The overwhelming tendency of modern global commerce today is the resort to offshore corporate vehicles without assets for trading purposes, making enforcement of judgments a difficult and frustrating exercise. In addition, it is very common that parties active in international commerce will elect to have their disputes resolved in leading centres (London, Paris, New York, etc) where neither party is physically present. Consequently at a very early stage, consideration must be given to the fundamental issue of how an award or judgment will be satisfied. This, in particular, includes the law on freezing order and other types of provisional (interim) measures focused upon in this work.

The authors have endeavoured to present an objective analysis of the solutions of four very different international jurisdictions to the typical problems encountered in this area. The fundamental cultural and social traditions of the two major common law countries and two civil law nations can explain the radically different treatment of some of the issues involved. The history and development of the relevant provisional arrest measures are examined for each jurisdiction attempting to highlight their advantages and possible failings. The result is, it is hoped, a broad panoramic spectrum presenting the existing legal solutions available to a potential creditor who wishes to secure his claim by arresting assets of his debtor before obtaining a final judgment.

As both the authors themselves come from quite different backgrounds, this may provide a more original perspective to the discussion of the issues involved. On the one hand, there are the pragmatic views of a dual qualified practising Anglo French lawyer, and on the other, the insight of a distinguished academic lawyer from Central Europe who also holds law degrees (LL.M. and S.J.D.) from the USA. It is thought that the text should be of interest to the graduate and postgraduate student as well as the practitioner.

It cannot be emphasised enough that the subject of this work has received surprisingly little attention to date from comparative lawyers. The authors sincerely hope that this pioneering study may encourage others to explore this field themselves in their own jurisdictions.

Last but not least, a word of gratitude to various institutions and persons who have been the source of inspiration for this co-authored monograph is due. Thus, Peter Iglikowski would like to express his gratitude to all the members of the Legal Studies Department of CEU including the postgraduate students who attended his lecture on 17 April 2013 as well as the trainee students from his postgraduate course at Paris V University who assisted him with the research. Professor Tajti would like to extend his thankfulness to Central European University (CEU), Budapest, for the support leading to this co-authored paper and specifically to the staff of CEU Library for their research-related assistance. Special thanks go also to Assistant Professor Jessica Lawrence (CEU) for the exchanges related to some parts of this monograph.

Paris, France/London, UK — Peter Iglikowski
Budapest, Hungary — Tibor Tajti (Thaythy)
April 2018

Contents

Chapter 1
Introduction

1.1 The Problem Stated and the Roadmap to the Monograph

This monograph compares the key characteristics of the laws of four representative legal systems on provisional measures with two interlinked goals. It not only aims to canvass the main comparative advantages or disadvantages of the observed systems but it also tries to answer the ultimate question of which of the analyzed remedies is best suited for the changed circumstances brought by the 21st century? The English Mareva Injunction, that is now known as a 'Freezing Order,' is taken as the benchmark to which each of the targeted systems' measures herein are primarily compared. This because according to English as well as scholars all over the world the Mareva Injunction forged by English lawyers is perceived not only as presumably the most effective provisional measure known today globally but is at the same time a real success story as well.[1]

Besides juxtaposing the quite widely discussed English and US law on provisional measures, this monograph uniquely adds not only the internationally less widely commented upon French *Saisie Conservatoire* but also the so far completely neglected offerings of Hungarian law. As a result we have four radically different approaches to provisional measures: English law positing injunctions as *in personam* relief in the forefront, French law instead relying on the *Saisie* with *in rem effects.* Lastly, Hungarian law represents out of the four the only system that has managed to survive without *ex parte* provisional measures so far. The analysis is then supplemented by a brief gloss on such recent related developments on the level of the European Union

[1] As Robert Goff eloquently phrased it in the foreword to the second edition of Hoyle's Freezing and Search Orders: "*That the Mareva jurisdiction is a success story is not in doubt. Its invention met a substantial need in [the UK]: its adoption in other common law countries shows that the need was as great for them as it was for us*." Hoyle (2006), foreword to the Second Edition at ix. For the fame Mareva acquired in the US, suffice to take a look at the cases and publications that follow the *Grupo Mexicano* case.

T. Tajti and P. Iglikowski, *A Cross Border Study of Freezing Orders and Provisional Measures*, SpringerBriefs in Law, https://doi.org/10.1007/978-3-319-94349-7_1

as the freshly introduced European Account Preservation Order or the 2016 *Rudolf Meroni v Recoletos Limited*[2] European Court of Justice judgment proclaiming the English Mareva Injunctions recognizable and enforceable.

In the light of that, the **Second Chapter** canvasses the history and main characteristics of the English Mareva Freezing Orders as compared to the French *Saisie Conservatoire.* It will be attempted to identify also those supplementary tools of each of these laws that make these provisional remedies efficient in practice. The **Third Chapter** dissects the tri-partite US system of significantly resembling yet still differing federal and State provisional measures. As US law relies on both *in rem* and *in personam* relief, it is a suitable model for comparison with the tandem of English and French law. What distinguishes it is that it places the *in rem* prejudgment attachments as the primary relief and the *in personam* preliminary injunctions only as supplementary relief destined for extraordinary circumstances.

As the **Fourth Chapter** shows, Hungary is a good contrast to the previous systems as far as *ex parte* relief is concerned given that it possesses none. This is in stark contrast not only to the maximally permissive English and French systems in which both the Mareva Injunction and the *Saisie Conservatoire* are as a rule issued without notifying the debtor, but also to the more restrictive American system. The **Fifth Chapter**—though together with scattered comments on European Union law in the monograph as well—contains a brief gloss on the present and future of the newly introduced European Account Preservation Order (EAPO).

It is hoped that the ensuing discussion will not only fill some gaps in comparative scholarship but will also perhaps become a valuable aid for all those developed and emerging systems all over the globe that are looking for guidance for improvement of their own systems.

1.2 Terminology Caveats

Unfortunately, the terminology on the central subject matter of this writing displays such significant differences, both as far as the English and various local language variants are concerned, that it requires special attention and comments to forestall misunderstandings. This seems to be inevitable whenever more than one legal system is compared as is the case herein. The variances then require careful selection of the key terms to be used in a comparative paper like this, and that may even occasionally require departures from the established usages in one or more of the observed jurisdictions. Here, such departures were brought to the minimum yet could not be excluded.

In the case of our topic two types of linguistic dilemmas were to be resolved: what phrase to use as the common denominator of all the laws covered and how to refer to or transpose to English the expressions used in the non-English language jurisdictions? While the latter concerned only France and Hungary, the quest for the common

[2]Judgment of the Court of First Chamber as of 25th of May 2016 in Case C-559/14.

denominator required not only reconciliation of English and US nomenclatures but also the English-versions of EU laws, keeping in sight as well the need to make the discussion on French or Hungarian law transparent and easy. The resulting multi-pronged language formula was based on the following facts and considerations.

First, as far as the common denominator was concerned, the phrase '**provisional measures**' was opted for because it seems to be that expression that fits most of the jurisdictions analysed by this paper and yet properly identifies the legal category in the center of our observations. Additionally, this was dictated also by the fact that the English Mareva Injunction—that is primarily referred to as a 'provisional' or 'interim'[3] measure—was set as the model to which all the other domestic law related concepts are compared. Title VIII of the US federal Rules of Civil Procedure also uses the near equivalent of 'provisional remedies,' covering both *in rem a*nd *in personal* measures (the latter including 'temporary restraining orders' which is an *ex parte* version of preliminary injunctions).

Therefore, the expression '**provisional measure**(s)' herein would encompass not only all variants of national interim (or interlocutory) measures but also the growing number of international variants as the European 'Account Preservation Order' (EAPO)[4] or 'provisional protective measures'[5] known to European conflicts of law. Further, our central term extends to both measures having *in rem* or *in personam* effect and irrespective of their denominations (e.g., the freezing and restraint orders of English law, or prejudgment remedies in US).

Secondly, when dealing with national laws, we will stick to the local nomenclature. Yet as division of provisional measures to those with *in rem* versus *in personam* effects plays a key role and as there are significant differences in the analysed laws in this respect, a pair of such terms was needed that would directly express these features of the provisional measures in question. Here, the US nomenclature was of help given that, as opposed to English law, it uses both *in rem* and *in personam* provisional measures. Hence, the common denominator for provisional measures having *in rem* effects will be '**preliminary attachments**,'[6] as opposed to provisional measures with *in personal* effects being referred to as '**preliminary injunctions**.'[7]

---

[3]See Briggs A. (2005), Chapter 6.03 captioned as "Interim Measures: the Freezing or Mareva injunction."

[4]See the related discussion in part 5 below.

[5]Art. 35 of the Regulation (EU) No. 1215/2012 of the European Parliament and of the Council of 12 December 2012 on jurisdiction and the recognition and enforcement of judgments in civil and commercial matters (recast).

[6]Some courts use the expression 'preliminary attachment' instead of 'prejudgment attachment.' See, e.g., *Prospect Communications v. Herman* [2013 WL 6276816] adjudicated by US District Court D. Minnesota [not reported in F.Supp.2d (2013)].

[7]Note that while Rule 65 of the federal Rules of Civil Procedure uses the exact expression of 'preliminary injunctions,' Rule 64 on *in rem* provisional remedies fails to add the attribute 'preliminary.' For this reason scholars refer to them normally as '**prejudgment** attachments' when it is of importance to stress this feature, what otherwise follows from the title VIII containing the rules on 'Provisional and Final Remedies.' See, e.g., Tabb J.Ch. & Brubaker R. (2003), at 40 *et seq.*; Wasserman R. (1992) at 268 *et seq.*; Barrack et al. (June 2011), at 52.

This is admittedly a departure from the familiar vocabulary of English lawyers that occasionally speak of the 'attachment' in connection with the Mareva Injunction as well.[8] This causes no problem for English law because in fact English law does not recognize provisional measures with *in rem* effect[9] (except with the special case of English maritime law, the Admiralty jurisdiction).[10] It is a problem, however, at the moment US law is added to the analysis, which has provisional measures with both *in rem* and *personam* effects as distinct remedies and for which this division is crucial. Moreover, as we shall see in the part on US law *infra*, the devices that are primarily available are the ones with *in rem* effects, the prototype of which is called exactly 'attachment,' to be distinguished from 'preliminary injunctions' that are awarded only exceptionally[11] and only with *in personam* effects.[12]

---

[8]See, for example, the following related excerpt from Roy Goode's *Commercial Law* (Penguin, 2nd ed., 1995) at 1166: "*The court can also order discovery and interrogatories in aid of the Mareva injunction for the purpose of ascertaining the existence and location of assets to which the injunction can attach,* though not for the purpose of ascertaining whether the defendant has committed a breach of the injunction." [Emphasis added.]

[9]See, e.g., Hess B. (2002), at 121.

[10]*See*, e.g., Tetley (June 1999), at 1955. This article is not concerned with admiralty law and hence this particular types of *in rem* remedy is not going to be discussed herein.

Otherwise, the list of interim remedies English courts are empowered to grant are listed in rule 25.1 of the Civil Procedure Rules (CPR). These do not include attachments that would create inchoate liens like the US prejudgment attachments. However, as one of the leading commentators cautiously added, the list "*is not necessarily an exhaustive list of the remedies that can be obtained [and] it is at least still arguable that a court may be prepared to devise a remedy, or make an adaptation of an existing remedy not specifically provided for, in order to facilitate its overall task of doing what procedural justice may require.*" In other words, there is a theoretical rather than realistic possibility that a court would invent an interim remedy not listed in the rules. Briggs, at 459.

[11]The US Supreme Court has reiterated its 'static approach' to preliminary injunctions in a series of post-Grupo Mexicano decisions, making these pre-judgment remedies extraordinary, "*a drastic provisional remedy that should be sparingly granted.*" DiSarro A. (2011), at 53.

[12]As a recent sample decision properly representing the approach US courts typically apply when deciding on TROs and preliminary injunctions see Civil No. 13 CV 578 (issued on 24th of January 2013 by US District Court for the Northern District of Illinois, Eastern Division) in the case between the *Federal Trade Commission* et al. *as plaintiffs and Fortune Hi-Tech Marketing Inc.* et al.

The court issued (among others) the Temporary Restraining Order (TRO) and 1/ordered the defendants and third parties holding assets of the defendants to refrain from disposing with them, 2/appointed a law firm as a temporary receiver to take full control of the Defendants, 3/"*defendants and their officers, agents, servants, employees, and attorneys, and all other persons in active concert of participation with any of them,*" if informed directly or indirectly about the court order, to cooperate with and hand over any property of the debtor held by them to the receiver, 4/repatriation of assets and documents in foreign countries, as well as 5/ expedited discovery.

In particular, the court not only set the expiration date of the TRO but also summoned the Defendant for a hearing "[...] *to show cause, if any, why [the] Court should not enter a preliminary injunction, pending final rule on the Complaint, against [the Defendants] enjoining them from further violations [of a number of federal and States statutes], continuing the freeze of their assets; making the temporary Receiver's appointment permanent, and imposing such additional relief as may be appropriate.*"

Thirdly, as we have already suggested above, given that in some of the targeted jurisdictions special well-established designations are in use, they are kept whenever that would not be detrimental to comprehension, and always with an explanation on the nature of such measures. For example, the French *Saisie Conservatoire* will primarily be referred to using the French designation, either the abbreviated '*Saisie*,' or its full version of '*Saisie Conservatoire*' instead of 'provisional attachments.' Likewise, the US temporary restraining order (TRO) will also be referred to under that particular designation. In the case of Hungary, which also has two provisional measures yet which deviate from the other discussed systems' devices considerably, we opted for metaphrasing combined with listing their key characteristics.

Fourthly, special emphasis is given to measures that could be awarded *ex parte* given that the existence or lack of such measures from a legal system increasingly is a matter of regulatory competition. Hungarian law, for example, essentially possesses no remedy with such effects as of yet. Moreover, notwithstanding that the *ex parte* nature of the Mareva Injunction or the French *saisie* is recognized as of key importance, normally these devices are not discussed or referred to under this particular heading. Consequently, the expression '*ex parte remedies*' would not be the most suitable as a common denominator for our purposes herein.

Last but not least, this terminology formula admittedly suffers from imperfections as well because it might suggest to the reader that the monograph is interested solely (or primarily) in what kinds of *provisional (interlocutory)* measures are offered by the observed systems as opposed to *final* procedural remedies? However, as already stated earlier, apart from this goal, the monograph has some additional very practical goals as well. In fact, the summit question, this paper tries to address is which of the laws offers not only the quickest remedy, ideally *ex parte* measures, but also in which system are such measures *realistically* within the reach of private parties? Such a focus obviously switches the emphasis on the *ex parte* or the preliminary nature of measures rather than on their non-final (provisional) facet. However, as normally, neither the *ex parte*, nor the preliminary nature, is the designation under which Mareva and the other discussed measures are usually described, the final verdict vouched for the selection of the 'provisional measures' variant.

References

EU Legislation

Regulation (EU) No. 1215/2012 of the European Parliament and of the Council of 12 December 2012 on jurisdiction and the recognition and enforcement of judgments in civil and commercial matters (recast)

Books

Briggs A Civil Jurisdiction and Judgments (2005) Norton Rose, London-Singapore
Goode R (1995) Commercial law, 2nd edn, Penguin
Hoyle MSW Freezing and Search Orders (2006) Informa-London, 4th ed
Tabb CJ, Brubaker R (2003) Bankruptcy law—principles, policies, and practice. Anderson Publications, Cincinnati

Articles

DiSarro A (2011) Freeze frame: the Supreme Court's reaffirmation of the substantive principles of preliminary injunctions. Gonzaga Law Rev 47(1):54–98
Tetley W (1999) Arrest, attachment, and related Maritime law procedures. Tulane Law Rev 73:1895–1985

Court Cases: European Union

Rudolf Meroni v Recoletos Limited, Judgment of the Court of First Chamber as of 25th of May 2016 (C-559/14)

Court Cases: United States

Civil No. 13 CV 578 (issued on 24th of January 2013 at 1:45 p.m. by US District Court for the Northern District of Illinois, Eastern Division) in the case between *the Federal Trade Commission et al. as plaintiffs and Fortune Hi-Tech Marketing Inc. et al.* as defendants. See at https://www.ftc.gov/sites/default/files/documents/cases/2013/01/130128fhtmtro.pdf
Prospect Communications v. Herman [2013 WL 6276816] adjudicated by US District Court D. Minnesota (not reported in F.Supp.2d (2013)

Internet Sources

Hess B (2002) Study No. JAI/A3/2002/02 on transparency of a Debtor's assets, attachment of bank accounts and provisional and protective measures. http://ec.europa.eu/civiljustice/publications/docs/enforcement_judicial_decisions_180204_en.pdf

Chapter 2
Provisional Measures in France and the United Kingdom

2.1 Background

The object of the first two sections of this monograph is to examine the differences between the law and procedure of England and France in relation to provisional measures to arrest assets or order a party to refrain from disposing of his assets. Such measures are commonly sought by parties to freeze assets in order that the party can enforce an eventual judgment for commercial claims. In the first part of this section the history and principal features of the English Freezing Order (Mareva Injunction) and the French *Saisie Conservatoire* are presented focusing on the differences between the two remedies. In the second part of the section consideration is given to the enforceability and recognition of English Freezing Orders and French *Saisies Conservatoires* in the European Union when the two remedies are being sought in relation to substantive proceedings to be brought in other European Union member states.

The English common law Mareva Injunction, now known as a Freezing Order,[1] and the French civil law *Saisie Conservatoire* are both remedies made available as provisional measures to creditors who face the risk that the assets of their debtor will be dissipated before they obtain an enforceable judgment. The institution of the *Saisie Conservatoire* has existed for a considerable period of time albeit in different forms.[1] By comparison the Mareva Injunction is a relatively novel concept[2] and is

[1]The existence of the right to arrest goods prior to a judgment, i.e., a *Saisie Conservatoire* has been recognized in France well before the great procedural reforms of the 19th and 20th Century codifying the rules for such remedies. The current rules in relation to the rights to obtain a *Saisie Conservatoire* were last significantly revised in important legislation in 1991: the Law of the 9th July 1991 (JO 14 Juillet p. 9228 and the Decree of the 31st of July 1992 (J0 5 août p. 10530). The relevant provisions have since been codified with minor amendments in the French Code of Civil Enforcement Procedure, which entered into force on 1st June 2012.

[2]It dates from the series of decisions of the Commercial Court and Court of Appeal beginning in 1975: besides the above cited Mareva case, the other key cases were *Nippon Yusen Kaisha*

T. Tajti and P. Iglikowski, *A Cross Border Study of Freezing Orders and Provisional Measures*, SpringerBriefs in Law, https://doi.org/10.1007/978-3-319-94349-7_2

an example of a quite radical judicial invention which was not without its critics in conservative legal circles when it first appeared.[3]

2.2 Definitions: The French *Saisie Conservatoire*

The *Saisie Conservatoire* allows an unpaid creditor to obtain the arrest (seizure) of assets belonging to his debtor in circumstances where he can demonstrate a good arguable case that he has a claim which is well founded and there is a serious risk that the claim will not be satisfied unless the attachment of the assets of the debtor are ordered. As such, sometimes it is also called a 'preventive seizure' ("*saisies à fin simplement conservatoire*").[4] The *Saisie Conservatoire*, albeit in different procedural forms, has traditionally been part of the institutional remedies available to a creditor against his debtor before he obtains a judgment or other order capable of enforcement. It is an important condition of obtaining such an arrest that the creditor must within a fixed time limit commence substantive legal proceedings on the merits against the debtor in order to obtain a judgment to enforce against the assets attached. The Order requires proceedings on the merits to be commenced against the debtor by the creditor within 30 days.[5] Once the order for attachment is granted by the Court the assets of the debtor are arrested and are in the absence of further court orders no longer available to the debtor. The rules governing the right to obtain a *Saisie Conservatoire* are currently to be found codified in the French Code of Civil Enforcement Procedures ("*Code des Procédures Civiles d'Exécution*").[6]

---

v Karageorgis (1975) 2 Lloyd's Law Reports 137 and *Rasu Maritima SA v Pertamina* (1977) 2 Lloyd's Rep. 397, CA.

[3]See, for example, Lord Hailsham's comments on the new injunctive remedy in the Siskina case (1978) 1 Lloyd's Rep. 1, HL at 9: "*Three years ago I would have regarded the respondents' case as wholly unarguable [...]. Now, however, this well established list of authorities, to the effect that an unsecured creditor cannot convert himself into a partially secured creditor merely by bringing an action against the alleged debtor and then seeking to freeze his assets by an injunction is, apparently, no longer reliable, at least as regards foreign based defendants with assets in this country [...].*"

[4]Bell et al (2008) at 117. As such it should be distinguished from other types of seizures (saisies), which are the products of the 1991–92 legislative reforms and which are not aimed merely to prevent dissipation of assets but amount already to enforcement itself. As far as the latter category is concerned, essentially different seizure proceedings apply to various classes of assets. Thus, one can distinguish seizure on the debtor's wages/salary ("*saisie des rémunérations du travail*") and seizure of real property ("*saisie immobilière*"). In case of chattels, two sub-types ought to be distinguished, one for enforcement on specific chattels and the other one aimed at restitution of specific corporeal assets ("*saisie revendications*" or "*saisie appréhensions*"). *Id.*

[5]Art R.511-7 of the *Code des Procédures Civiles d'Exécution, Livre Cinquième les Mesures Conservatoires* (Edition Dalloz, 104th ed. 2013).

[6]Text of the Code in French available at <https://www.legifrance.gouv.fr/affichCode.do?cidTexte=LEGITEXT000025024948>. [Accessed 10 April 2018].

2.2.1 Saisie Conservatoire *in Comparison to the* Référé

Given that the *Saisie Conservatoire* is an *in rem* provisional remedy and thus it is not the full equivalent of the English Mareva Injunction or the Freezing Order, it ought to be mentioned that in personam provisional orders may also be issued in France in the so-called *référé proceedings*.[7] However, as we are focusing in this writing on the *Saisie* as the most popular French provisional remedy, only the most important features of the *référé* are canvassed here.

The jurisdiction of the *juge des référés* corresponds broadly to what English lawyers refer to as the powers of an interlocutory judge. The distinction is essentially between the jurisdiction of a judge who can determine the merits of a dispute and a judge whose powers are limited to taking urgent provisional steps to preserve the rights of the parties before a judgment on the merits. Article 484 of the French Code of Civil Procedure defines a decision of a *juge des référés* as a provisional measure taken for urgent steps which are necessary. Article 493 of the Code of Civil Procedure authorizes the *juge des référés* to make such orders without notice being given by the Claimant to the other party if the urgency of the cause requires. The *référé* system only allows the judge to make provisional orders to protect the interests of the parties but the *juge des référés* has no jurisdiction to determine the merits or substance of the dispute.

In fact, the procedure for applications for a *Saisie Conservatoire* will be the *référé* system where the claimant petitioner can seek an order without notice to the other party. The judge (*juge des référés*) will grant a Saisie Conservatoire as an urgent provisional measure pending the final decision of the court or judge who will determine the substance of the matter. In proceedings where the *référé* system is applied the normal time limits for service of legal summons and submissions are not observed. In view of the urgency the parties can serve very short notice of an application to hear a petition to the *juge des référés*. When a creditor seeks an order for a *Saisie Conservatoire* the procedural rules of the *référé* system are effectively applied. That means that the creditor can obtain the order for a *Saisie Conservatoire ex parte* without notice to the debtor though the debtor will be entitled to seek an urgent hearing at very short notice before the court to hear an application to lift the arrest.

---

[7]Note that *référé* proceedings exist in two different types of procedural laws in French law: while we are interested solely in the ones forming part of civil procedure law ("*l'ordre judiciare*"), *référé* proceedings exist also in administrative law ("*l'ordre administratif*"). The latter are fast forms of judicial review of administrative acts. Today, more such administrative *référés* are available to citizens. For example, the function of the "*référé-suspension*" is fast suspension of the implementation of an administrative act but is "*conditioned by a degree of urgency and the existence of serious doubt as to the legality of the [attacked] administrative decision.*" As opposed to that the "*référé-conservatoire*" aims to freeze the "*factual circumstances if these are likely to disappear because of the performance of administrative activity.*" These play an increasingly important role as forms of judicial review of administrative acts as due to the doctrine of '*décision exécutoire*' administrative decisions are enforced even if challenged unless a court orders otherwise. Bell et al. (2008), at 123.

However, the right to resort to the powers of a *juge des référés* to seek an urgent order and the right of a creditor to seek a *Saisie Conservatoire* are distinct matters even though in practice the procedural rules governing the applications are very similar. In the *référé* system the judge has the power to make a provisional order which he considers appropriate to preserve the interests of the parties. Theoretically that could mean that the judge could issue an injunction *in personam* to the debtor ordering him to refrain from disposing of his assets following the model of the Mareva Injunction Freezing Order. But in practice that would not occur because French law, unlike English law, recognizes the right of a creditor to seek a pre judgment arrest: a *Saisie Conservatoire*. The *référé* system would be used typically by a party to seek an urgent provisional measure ordering the other party to refrain from conduct causing him prejudice until the merits of the substantial action are tried. Therefore the French *référé* system corresponds to the jurisdiction of the English courts to grant interlocutory injunctions but will not be invoked by the French court to grant to grant an *in personam* restraining injunction to freeze assets. Instead the creditor needs to seek a *Saisie Conservatoire*.

2.3 Definitions: The English Mareva Injunction or Freezing Order

The Mareva Injunction or Freezing Order is a relatively novel judicial remedy which was developed entirely at the initiative of the English courts and prior to its invention had no existence in common law or statute. Traditionally English common law, unlike French civil law, had not accepted that a claimant could seek to arrest or restrain the disposal of assets by his debtor before obtaining a judgment. The position of common law was that there was no right to seek an injunction to restrain a defendant from disposing of his assets before a judgment on the merits of the action was obtained. Lord Hailsham in an early case dealing with the newly introduced Mareva injunction thus stressed that "*[t]he only remedy for a creditor in that case (i.e. an unsecured creditor) is to obtain his judgment and take out execution.*"[8]

The Mareva Injunction was a departure from this principle and the previous common law authorities were distinguished on the grounds that they did not deal with the situation where a foreign based debtor was being restrained from removing his assets from the jurisdiction to frustrate the enforcement of a judgment. The injunction was first invoked in a series of cases before the Commercial Court and Court of Appeal in 1975[9] before the eminent commercial judge Lord Denning.

The second case involved a vessel called the Mareva which gave the name to the injunction. Since the reform of the English procedural system and introduction of the Civil Procedure Rules (CPR) the remedy has been classified as an interim injunction

[8] *Siskina, The. Owners of Cargo Lately Laden on Board the Siskina v. Distos Compania Naviera SA* [1979] AC 210; (1978) 1 Lloyds Law Reports [hereinafter: Siskina 1978].

[9] See note 17 supra.

called a Freezing Order. In support of the new remedy Lord Denning relied on statutory law[10] giving the courts a wide discretion to grant an interlocutory injunction whenever it appears to the courts to be just and convenient. Such injunctions were granted to allow the courts to make provisional orders to preserve the rights of parties where there is a risk that their rights will be prejudiced in the absence of a restraining order. It was on this basis that Lord Denning considered that the courts could allow a Claimant to restrain a debtor from removing his assets from the jurisdiction on the grounds that otherwise the removal of the assets would prevent the creditor from being able to enforce a judgment. Moreover, more freezing order can be ordered against the same person "*in each of two or more different proceedings*."[11]

Prior to the above mentioned decisions of the Commercial Court and its subsequent approval by the Court of Appeal the English courts had never allowed a Claimant without an enforceable judgment to obtain the detention of the assets of a debtor. The distinctive feature of the Mareva Injunction is that it does not involve an attachment of assets as such but is simply a court order enforceable against the debtor *in personam*[12] restraining him from removing or interfering with the assets in question. The assets themselves are not arrested or attached and in the event of a breach of the injunction by the debtor the remedy of the Claimant will be an action against the Debtor for contempt of court in refusing to comply with the order. The remedy is therefore essentially an order effective *in personam* against the debtor and not an order *in rem* attaching to property or chattels, in contrast with either the French *Saisie* or the US prejudgment attachments.

Since its beginnings in 1975, the law in relation to the circumstances in which such an injunction will be allowed has been considerably expanded. It is perhaps the single most important development in English commercial law practice in the last thirty years.[13]

---

[10] See section 45 of the Supreme Court of Judicature (Consolidation) Act 1925. Note that this act was repealed by the Senior Courts Act 1981 (originally named 'the Supreme Court Act 1981'). Section 45 of this act provided: "*A mandamus or injunction may be granted or a receiver appointed by an interlocutory order of the court in all cases in which it shall appear to the court to be just or convenient.*" *See also* Hoyle (2006), para 1.7., at 3 and Davies P.S. & Virgo G. (2013), at 943.

[11] See, e.g., Gee S.Q.C. (2016), para 21-036, at 752. In such cases, each freezing order will have a "*maximum sum calculated by reference to the claim in those proceedings.*" To ensure clarity and precision, in such cases it should be stated by explicit language that "*the defendant is restrained from dealing with his assets within the jurisdiction save in so far as these exceed the aggregate of the maximum sum and the sum which the defendant is enjoined from dealing with under the other injunction.*" Id.

[12] As Gee S. Q.C. (2016), para 1-029, at 23 put it: "*A Mareva injunction imposes restraint on the conduct of the person enjoined and does not operate in rem on an asset.*"

[13] See Eder B. Sir (2013) at 47: "*I would suggest that it [ie the Mareva Injunction] is probably the single most important development affecting shipping disputes over the last 30 years.*"

2.4 The Basic Problem: Locating a Debtor's Assets and Preventing Their Removal

A Claimant will clearly be concerned at an early stage in any dispute to ensure that any judgment obtained for his claim will be satisfied by the Debtor. The most common practice for a Claimant to protect himself against the risk of an unsatisfied judgment is to seek to arrest or attach any known assets of his Debtor before obtaining a judgment. Such an attachment will also in practice exert pressure on the Debtor to make proposals to resolve the dispute although this should not properly be the object of the arrest application. Typically a successful arrest of an asset will induce the Debtor to provide security in the form of a bank guarantee to obtain release of the assets. Conversely, a debtor, particularly if he is not acting in good faith will seek to remove his assets from jurisdictions where they can be readily attached. In the case of the risk of exposure to substantial claims the debtor may even seek to conceal his assets using complex corporate structures in different jurisdictions.

The procedural remedy of the *Saisie Conservatoire* will allow a Claimant to arrest or attach assets if he knows where they are located. But the English courts have increasingly expanded the range of ancillary remedies available to unpaid creditors against their debtors to allow them to obtain court orders which oblige the Debtor to reveal where his assets are located in addition to injunctions restraining a debtor from dissipating assets even where they are located outside the jurisdiction of the English courts. Such orders may, if justified, include Disclosure Orders[14] obliging the debtor or an officer of the debtor to disclose information about the presence of assets within or outside the jurisdiction, i.e. worldwide. In the Court of Appeal decision of 1988 *Babanaft*[15] such orders were confirmed. It has become quite common practice since then for courts to grant similar Disclosure Orders which may require a Debtor to make a statement as to the presence of his assets worldwide.[16]

[14]As Gee S.Q.C. (2016), para 1-044, at 31, "*[the disclosure order is] sometimes more important than the injunction because it aids the process of enforcement by identifying assets against which enforcement can be had.*"

[15]*Babanaft International Co. S.A v Bahaedine Bassatne and Walid Mohamed Bassatne* [1990] Ch 13; [1988] 2 Lloyds Law Reports 435, CA.

[16]For a recent decision on the criteria to be considered when granting such orders see *Royal Bank of Scotland v FAL Oil Co Ltd* [2012] 1 Lloyds Law Reports 327.

2.5 The Mareva Injunction or Freezing Order

2.5.1 Historical Origins of the Freezing Order or Mareva Injunction

Before 1975 it was accepted as a matter of English legal practice that prior to obtaining a judgment an unpaid creditor had no rights to seek to arrest or attach the assets of his debtor.[17] The procedure of attachment or *Saisie Conservatoire* prevalent on the continent in civil law jurisdictions, or the US prejudgment attachments, had no equivalent in the English courts. Such orders were occasionally sought but systematically refused on the grounds of an absence of any inherent jurisdiction of the English courts to grant such relief. History was made when in two landmark maritime cases in 1975 the Commercial Court in London,[18] supported on appeal by the Court of Appeal presided by Lord Denning, allowed an unpaid creditor to obtain a prejudgment order (relying on the inherent jurisdiction of the English courts under the 1925 Supreme Court of Judicature Act section 45)[19] to issue an injunction restraining a defendant from certain conduct if it appeared just and convenient to the Court. Lord Denning distinguished the earlier line of English legal authorities barring such a remedy[20] by pointing out that those cases did not deal with the situation where a defendant was out of the jurisdiction but had money in the UK.[21]

In both cases ship owners were seeking to attach assets of a charterer of a vessel for unpaid hire due to the ship owners under the charter party. In initially brief judgments the Court justified the interference with the defendants' goods within the jurisdiction on the ground that if the defendant was not restrained by a court order ("the injunction") from removing the assets from the jurisdiction then the Creditor's claim would not be satisfied upon obtaining a judgment. The vessel involved in the second case was the Mareva which gave the name to the new procedural device: the Mareva Injunction. The legal reasoning of the court expanded principally by the

[17]See, for example, Lord Denning in *Nippon Yusen Kaisha v Karageorgis* (1975) LLR 137 at 138: "*We are told that an injunction of this kind has never been done before. It has never been the practice of the English courts to seize assets of a defendant in advance of judgment or to restrain the disposal of them.*"

[18]*Nippon Yusen Kaisha v. Karageorgis and another* [1975] 1 WLR 1093, CA (22 May 1975) Lord Denning MR, Browne and Geoffrey Lawn LJJ and *Mareva Compania Naviera SA v. International Bulkcarriers SA* [1975] 2 Lloyd's Rep. 509, CA (23 June 1975; Lord Denning MR, Roskill and Ormrod LJJ.

[19]Section 45 has now been replaced by S.37 (1) of the Supreme Court Act 1981 which provides that "*The High Court may by order (whether interlocutory or final) grant an injunction...in all cases in which it appears just and convenient to the court to do so.*"

[20]*Lister v Stubbs* (1890) 45 Ch.D 1 at 14 and *Burmester v Burmester* (1913) p. 76 at 79 and Lord Justice Scrutton in *Jagger v Jagger* (1926) at 93 and 102.

[21]*Rasu Maritime SA* v *Pertamina* [1977] 2 LLR 397 at 402.

eminent commercial judge Lord Denning was that the courts always had an inherent power to make orders if it were just and convenient to preserve the interests of parties before a judgment had been obtained.[22]

The source of the legal foundation for this new device was in the rules developed by the English branch of law known as Equity governing the granting of injunctions. But the legitimacy of the new injunction created by these decisions was a source of controversy in conservative circles in England.[23] The learned authors of one leading work on Equity even cast doubt on the source of equity claimed to establish the remedy.[24] In the course of his pioneering judgment in Rasu Maritima in 1975, the third case in which the novel remedy was discussed in further detail, Lord Denning drew analogies between the Mareva Injunction and the continental *Saisie Conservatoire* referring to an alleged practice existing in the seventeenth century in London and other mercantile cities allowing the assets of foreign parties to be arrested.[25] Lord Denning observed that now that the United Kingdom had become a member of the European Union it was appropriate for it to adapt its legal system to have similar legal remedies available to litigants as the continental law *Saisie Conservatoire* known to the civil law courts. By contrast, it is interesting to note that the US Supreme Court in its decision in the *Grupo Mexicano* case[26]—as we will see below in more detail—decided not to follow the example of the Mareva Injunction considering that there was no authority for the right to invoke such an order and that it would be appropriate for the US Congress to decide whether such a legal remedy should be brought into existence.[27]

---

[22] *Id.* at 402 where Lord Denning cites S.45 of the Judicature Act in support of the principal that an injunction may be granted in all cases in which it shall appear to the court to be just and convenient.

[23] See the Siskina (1978) 1 LLR at 9 where Lord Hailsham points to the illogicality of allowing Mareva Injunctions against foreign based defendants with money in England in the Commercial Court whereas a similar remedy is not available to a Claimant pursuing an English based Defendant in the High Court: "*In any event it is clear that the Mareva injunctions cannot be allowed to flourish independently in the arcadia of the commercial list without being applied in the High Court generally in all cases where plaintiffs and defendants are comparably placed.*"

[24] Gummow M. and Lehane (2003), par 21-435 at 798: "*In truth, there is no jurisdiction to grant a Mareva Injunction*" cited with disapproval by Gee S. in his article the Undertaking in Damages in 2006 LMCLQ at page 187.

[25] See *Rasu Maritima SA v Pertamina* (1977) 2 LLR 397 at 401: "*I would like first to give a historical and comparative survey as to this procedure of seizure of assets before trial or judgment…In former times it was much used in the city of London by a process called foreign attachment […].*"

[26] *Grupo Mexicano de Desarollo v Alliance Bond Fund Inc.* [527 US 308 (1990)].

[27] In its reasoning the US Supreme Court noted that the English Court of Chancery (sic) did not provide a pre-judgment injunctive remedy until 1975, and the decision doing so has been viewed by commentators as a dramatic departure from prior practice. Enjoining the debtor's disposition of his property at the instance of a non judgment creditor is incompatible with this Court's traditionally cautious approach to equitable powers, which leaves any substantial expansion of practice to Congress. See also the section on US provisional remedies.

2.5.2 *The Key Characteristics of the Mareva Injunction*

The essential characteristic of the new Mareva Injunction was that it was an extension of the power of the courts to issue interlocutory injunctions which could include an order restraining a defendant from removing or dissipating his assets to frustrate the enforcement of an ultimate judgment against him. In the course of the development of this new area of the law the courts maintained that the equitable rules applying to the grant of the injunction governed the underlying principles behind the remedy. Several important characteristics of the Mareva Injunction were a consequence of this principle.

Most importantly the courts insisted that the power to grant a Mareva Injunction was discretionary and not a right. The courts had to look at the individual circumstances of each case in order to determine whether it was appropriate and just to grant the injunction. The following conditions were identified as being essential for the Mareva Injunction to be given:

- *Firstly* the Claimant had to show a good arguable case that his claim against the Debtor was well founded.
- *Secondly,* the Claimant had to demonstrate that there was a serious risk that a judgment would not be enforced because the Debtor was seeking to dissipate his assets by removing them from the jurisdiction in order to frustrate the Claimant's endeavors to recover the debt.
- *Thirdly*, as the remedy involved was historically a creation of the English branch of the law known as Equity the court insisted that the remedy would only be available to parties who had not been guilty of any misconduct or impropriety. This because according to the old adage parties who seek relief from the law of Equity have to come to the courts with 'clean hands.'[28]
- *Fourthly,* it followed from this principle that it was essential that the would-be-Claimant had to make full and frank disclosure of all issues relevant to his application including any arguments or circumstances which could persuade a court not to grant the order. The failure to make such full and frank disclosure could, it was a matter of discretion for the court, allow the court to discharge any order originally granted. Such applications would always be made *ex parte* that is without notice to the other party. Hence the importance that the Claimant did nothing which could mislead the court. The importance of this principle can be illustrated by a judgment in 2017 (unreported as of the time of writing this monograph) of the High Court approving the decision of a disciplinary tribunal striking off (i.e.

[28]The injunction is historically regarded as equitable relief. The branch of the law known as Equity in England was developed essentially on equitable and just principles to mitigate the rigours of the common law. The courts of the Lord Chancellor were historically the courts which applied the law of equity and the courts of the King dealt with the common law. It was in the great reforms of the 19th Century in 1875 that the two court systems were fused allowing equitable remedies to be applied by common law judges. It has long been regarded by tradition that any one seeking equitable relief must come to equity with clean hands.

barring from practice) a solicitor who had omitted to make proper disclosure of material issues in an affidavit in support of a Freezing Order.

- *Finally*, once again as a consequence of the fact that the remedy was an interlocutory injunction to preserve parties' rights before judgment, the Claimant would always be obliged to give the court an undertaking that in the event the court decides that the Order should not have been granted then the Claimant will indemnify the Defendant and any third parties who have suffered damage as a result of the granting of the injunction.[29] It has been the practice of the courts when granting injunctions without notice to the other side (*ex parte*) that the Claimant must always give an undertaking (known as an undertaking in damages) to the court to indemnify the Defendant in the event that the relief sought was not justified or the claim fails. Such an undertaking may require to be fortified by a bank guarantee or other security in the discretion of the court.[30] The Mareva and subsequently Freezing Order was classified from the outset as an injunction and hence the undertaking in damages was required.[31] Where the Claimant is not a substantial asset owning company a Defendant may seek for the undertaking in damages to be fortified by an appropriate guarantee from a bank or other institution in the discretion of the judge for example a holding company if a subsidiary is involved.

2.5.3 Expansion of the Scope of Mareva Injunctions and Freezing Orders

Initially the courts restricted the granting of Mareva Injunctions to legal proceedings on the merits to be pursued before the English courts. But the jurisdiction was extended to include proceedings before the courts of EU member states under the 1982 Civil Jurisdiction and Judgment Act.[32] Subsequently, pursuant to a statutory instrument in 1997, the jurisdiction to grant Freezing Orders was further extended to proceedings before other foreign courts.[33]

The ability of the English courts to grant such injunctions was widely recognized by the international legal community as a very significant development given the prominence of London in international trade. Consequently the Commercial Court in London began to devote an ever increasing proportion of its resources to the exercise of this new power. In the course of the development of this area of the law the courts progressively increased the ancillary powers of the courts to grant further

[29] As to the requirement for the undertaking *see generally* Gee S. (2006), at 181.

[30] See *Energy Ventures Partners Ltd v Malabu Oil & Gas Ltd* [2014 EWCA Civ1295] for a discussion in the Court of Appeal on the criteria to justify a request from a defendant for fortification.

[31] *Nippon Yusen Kaisha v Karageorgis* [1975] 1 WLR 1093; [1975] 2 Lloyds Law Reports 137, CA.

[32] See section 25 of the Civil Jurisdiction and Judgments Act 1982 which conferred the power to grant interim injunctions including freezing orders in support of proceedings brought before a Brussels Convention contracting state.

[33] Civil Jurisdiction and Judgments Act 1982 (Interim Relief) Order 1997.

orders to make the Mareva Injunctions more effective including orders obliging a debtor to make disclosure of his assets both within and outside the jurisdiction.

It became consequently more common for the courts granting Mareva Injunctions to make related orders obliging the Defendant debtor or its officers to make disclosure to the court as to the existence or location of its assets irrespective of whether these assets were within or outside the jurisdiction. In landmark decisions in the 1980s[34] the courts even held that in exceptional cases the court could grant a worldwide Mareva Injunction freezing the assets of the Defendant both inside and outside of the English jurisdiction. In its decision in the widely publicised *Republic of Haiti versus Duval* case the court gave orders freezing assets worldwide as well as requiring the Defendant to make disclosure of their assets. Subsequently in the litigation involving the *Babanaft group*[35] the Court of Appeal, reversing a decision of a Commercial Court judge, approved the extension of Mareva Injunctions to assets worldwide. Since those decisions the courts have continued to develop their jurisdiction to grant worldwide Freezing Orders and ancillary relief.

In the course of the development of this area of the law the courts focused on the principles which should be respected when granting worldwide freezing orders in support of foreign litigation or arbitration proceedings. In particular the courts decided that when considering whether to grant a worldwide freezing order in support of foreign litigation certain rules should be followed to examine whether in all the circumstances it would be inexpedient to make the order.[36] Recent decisions of the courts have further explored the principles to be followed in the exercise of the court's discretion to grant such worldwide freezing orders. For example in the Court of Appeal decision in *Dadourian Group International Inc v Simms*[37] and the Commercial Court judgment in the case of *Royal Bank of Scotland PLC v FAL Oil Co Ltd*[38] the courts embarked on quite lengthy examinations of the guidelines which should be observed.

The relevant principles can be summarised as follows. When the English court is considering granting a worldwide freezing order over assets of a Defendant who may be domiciled or resident in England but where substantive proceedings are contemplated before foreign courts the following principles should apply.

- Firstly, the court had to consider whether the facts would warrant the relief sought if the substantive proceedings had been brought in England (this would normally involve examining whether the Claimant had a good arguable case and there was a serious risk of dissipation of assets).
- Secondly, if the answer to that question was affirmative then the court had to consider whether the fact that the court had no jurisdiction apart from the relevant

[34] See *Republic of Haiti v Duvalier* (1989) 1 LLR 111 and *Babanaft International Co SA v Bassatne* (1988) 2 LLR 435.

[35] *Babanaft International Co SA v Bassatne* (1988) 2 LLR 435.

[36] See, for example, *Credit Suisse Fides Trust SA v Cuoghi* (1998) QB 818; [1997] 3 WLR 871, CA and *Motorola Credit Corporation v Uzan* [2003] EWCA Civ 752 (2004) 1 WLR 113, CA.

[37] *Dadourian Group International Inc. v Simms* (2006) Lloyd's Rep. 2 354; EWCA Civ. 399, CA.

[38] *Royal Bank of Scotland PLC v Fal Oil Ltd and others* (2013) 1 Lloyd's Rep 327.

section made it inexpedient to grant the relief. The court then suggested that there would be five particular considerations which should be examined as to the issue of whether it would be inexpedient to grant the relief:

1. Whether the making of the order by the English court would interfere with the management of the case in the primary foreign court where the substantive proceedings were being pursued.
2. Whether it was the policy of the primary foreign jurisdiction not to make worldwide freezing/disclosure orders. If not, the English court should consider whether making such an order would be proper and not interfere with the powers of the foreign jurisdiction and principles of international comity generally.
3. Whether there was a danger that the orders made would give rise to disharmony or confusion and/or risk of conflicting inconsistent or overlapping orders in other jurisdictions in particular before the courts of the state where the person enjoined resided or where the assets affected were located. If so then respect for the territorial jurisdiction of that state should discourage the English court from using its unusually wide powers against a foreign defendant.
4. Whether at the time the order was sought there was likely to be a potential conflict as to jurisdiction rendering it inappropriate and inexpedient to make a worldwide order, and
5. Whether in a case where jurisdiction was resisted and disobedience to be expected, the court would be making an order which it could not enforce.

This radical extension of the powers of the English courts to make worldwide freezing and disclosure orders has inevitably attracted attention in relation to the compatibility of such orders with respect and comity for foreign courts.[39] In particular concern has been raised that the European Court of Justice (ECJ) may be invited to express views as to the appropriateness of such orders in the context of the recognition and enforcement of judgments in the EU and under regulation 44/2001. The recent decisions of the ECJ[40] in connection with the practice of the English courts to issue anti-suit injunctions has given rise to further concern that a similarly rigid approach may be adopted in so far as member courts of the EU are concerned. This is discussed further below.

2.6 The *Saisie Conservatoire*

2.6.1 A Brief Legislative History of the Saisie Conservatoire

In comparison to the Mareva Injunction or Freezing Order the institution of the *Saisie Conservatoire* is firmly established and relatively straightforward in its operation and

[39] See, for example, Louise Merrett L. (2008), 71 and Sainte Rose J. (10 Febr. 2005), at 237.

[40] *Turner v Gromit Case* (C-159/02) and the decision of the ECJ of the 10th February 2009 in *Front Comor West Tankers Inc v Allianz SPA* (C-185/07).

effects. The legal rules relating to the jurisdiction of the French courts to grant a *Saisie Conservatoire* were restated and defined in the law no 91-650 of the 9 July 1991 and the decree no 92 of -755 of the 31 July 1991. But these legal provisions are essentially revised versions of the previous existing laws which had long accepted the principle that a Creditor with a good prima facie claim had a right to arrest the assets of his debtor where there was a risk that the claim would not be satisfied without such a measure. The rules set out in the law and decree of 1991 were subsequently set out in a new codified form in the *Code des Procedures Civiles D'Execution* were they are now to be found at Articles L 511-1 and following Article R.511-1 and ff for the law and decree respectively. This codified statement of the essential rules relating to the *Saisie Consevatoire* with minor amendments dates from 2012.[41] The legislation of 1991 reformed the rules governing the right to obtain a *Saisie Conservatoire* in place of the previous rules notably article 48 of the former Code of Civil Procedure.

In particular the legislation introduced an important innovation: the jurisdiction of the *Juge de l'Execution* (the JEX is the judge responsible for the enforcement of legal decisions) who would be competent to determine all issues and disputes arising out of an order authorising a *Saisie Conservatoire*.[42] Prior to that, important legislation in 1955[43] had reformed and simplified the rules in relation to the *Saisie Conservatoire* making them more appropriate to the changed circumstances of commerce since the nineteenth century. The concept of a right to arrest assets of a debtor before a judgment has been obtained has long formed part of the traditional remedies available as a matter of French civil law even though the variety and forms of the attachment gave rise to some confusion before the reforms of the twentieth century.

2.6.2 The Key Characteristics of the Saisie Conservatoire

The *Saisie Conservatoire* is fundamentally an arrest or attachment of assets of a debtor prior to the obtaining of a judgment. The granting of such a *Saisie Conservatoire* has the effect of immobilising the assets concerned which are no longer available to the debtor.[44] An essential distinction between the French *Saisie Conservatoire* and the Mareva Injunction is that the former involves *actual arrest and seizure* of the asset concerned whereas the Mareva Injunction is *only an order* restraining the debtor or other third party holding assets from disposing of them without authorization from the court. In that sense the *Saisie Conservatoire* would be categorized in English legal terms as an *in rem* remedy while the Mareva Injunction is solely an *in personam* remedy. It has long been established by French civil law that a claimant who can

[41]The relevant provisions of the Law no 91-650 of the 9th July 1991 and the Decree no 92-755 of the 31st of July 1992 have now been codified in the 5th book of the *Code des Procédures Civiles d'Exécution* (CPCE) 2012 dealing with interim measures or "*mesures conservatoires*."

[42]Article 69 of the Law no 91-650 of the 9th July 1991, now Art. L511-3 CPCE.

[43]The Law of the 12 November 1955 introduced the right to obtain a *Saisie Conservatoire générale*.

[44]Arts. L. 521-1 and L. 523-1 CPCE.

establish a good arguable case for a valid claim which may not be satisfied in the absence of an attachment is entitled to seek an order from the court seizing the assets of his debtor prior to obtaining a judgment.

There are three distinctive features of the *Saisie Conservatoire* which clearly differentiate it from the Mareva Injunction. *Firstly,* as already indicated above, it is an attachment or arrest of assets and not simply an injunction ordering a debtor to refrain from removing or dissipating assets. Pursuant to Article L 521-1 of the *Code des Procedures Civiles d'Execution* the effect of a *Saisie Conservatoire* is to render the assets arrested unavailable to the Debtor or party which holds them. Important property rights available to the creditor may result from this distinction which are considered further below. *Secondly,* the relevant legislation and articles of the French Code of Civil Enforcement Procedures (CPCE) make it clear that the creditor has a right to seek attachment of assets if the conditions required are satisfied. The remedy is not discretionary as in the case of the Mareva Injunction. *Thirdly,* the French Court must of course determine on the basis of the evidence presented that the Claimant has made out a case for obtaining the *Saisie Conservatoire*, i.e. there is a valid claim and a danger that it will not be satisfied. But beyond that the French Court does not have a discretion to exercise in terms of whether it would be just and equitable to grant the relief sought. It follows that the restrictive conditions imposed by the English courts in granting Freezing Orders (e.g., the requirement to give an undertaking in damages and the necessity to make full and frank disclosure) are not relevant to applications to seek a *Saisie Conservatoire*.

It follows from the important feature of the *Saisie Conservatoire* making it an attachment of assets that the successful Claimant obtaining a *Saisie Conservatoire* of his debtor's assets may also obtain certain priority rights over the goods attached. In particular Article L 523-1 of the *Code des Procedures Civiles d'Execution* provides that the conservative attachment of the amounts in question has the same effect as defined by Article 2350 of the French Civil Code giving the Creditor a preferred claim (i.e., priority) over the assets arrested in preference to other creditors. Article 2350 combined with Article 2333 of the Civil Code allow a Creditor who has obtained a *Saisie Conservatoire* over assets to be in the same position as a secured creditor over pledged goods. The detailed consideration of the secured rights of Creditors following a *Saisie Conservatoire* and whether they can take priority over other creditors in the event of insolvency proceedings would require detailed consideration of each different set of facts involved and is beyond the scope of this monograph. By contrast the Mareva Injunction Freezing Order does not give rise to any property rights conferred upon the creditor in relation to the assets affected by the Order.

2.7 The Procedure for Obtaining a *Saisie Conservatoire* and Mareva Injunction Freezing Order

2.7.1 The Procedure for Obtaining the Saisie Conservatoire

Article L. 511-1, par 1 of the CPCE provides that: "*Any person whose claim appears to be well founded in principle can seek authorisation from a judge to exercise a conservative attachment order over the goods of his debtor without a previous executive title if it can justify circumstances susceptible of preventing recovery of its claim*". In the corresponding article R. 511-1, par 1 and following CPCE, it is stated that: "*The authorisation provided for in article L. 511-1 is requested by petition.*" The request for a conservative attachment is presented by way of summons before the court where the debtor resides.

The legislation of 1991 and 1992 introduced the jurisdiction of the *juge de l'éxécution* (from the Tribunal de Grande Instance), or judge responsible for enforcement, who would normally be the judge to whom applications for conservative attachments of goods should be made. But the law additionally provides that the President of the Tribunal de Commerce or the President of the Commercial Court may also have jurisdiction to grant conservative attachment orders where no substantive proceedings have yet been commenced in relation to the claim.[45] The court which will have territorial jurisdiction to hear applications for conservative arrests will be the court of the domicile of the debtor (or the court of the place where the interim order is to be carried out if the debtor resides abroad or if his domicile is unknown).[46]

The practice is for the claimant to make an application *ex parte* before the judge i.e. without summoning the Debtor to be present. The Creditor will have to present a petition to the court with evidence demonstrating that the conditions required for granting a *Saisie Conservatoire* have been met: i.e. essentially a good arguable case in principle and the risk that the claim will not be paid.[47] Unlike the Mareva Injunction or the Freezing Order, granting of the *Saisie Conservatoire* is, however, not in the discretion of the judge. Rather, the French court has to be satisfied "merely" that the evidence presented justifies the remedy to issue it. If the court grants the arrest then the Claimant will obtain an Order or Ordonnance which must then be served on the Debtor and or third party if the assets are held by a bank or other financial institution. The order will have to be served by a Court Bailiff or *Huissier* on the Debtor and/or third party. The effect of the service of the order on the Debtor will be to arrest the assets in question which will no longer be available to the Debtor. The costs of enforcing the arrest order will normally be borne by the Debtor but where

---

[45]Decree no 92-755 of the 31st July 1992 art. 211 and art. 69.1 of the Law no 91-650 of the 9th July 1991, now art. L. 511-3 CPCE.

[46]Arts. R. 511-2 and R. 121-2 CPCE.

[47]Art. L.511-1 CPCE.

the arrest order is lifted by the court then the Claimant may if appropriate be held liable to indemnify the loss caused by the arrest.[48]

The law also requires that the Court Bailiff within eight days of executing the order must serve upon the Debtor and/or third party holding the assets a *procès verbal* or protocol recording the attachment of the assets and service of the order.[49] It is also an imperative condition of the granting of the *Saisie Conservatoire* that the Creditor must commence substantive proceedings on the merits against the Debtor within one month of the date of the order in order to obtain an enforceable judgment or title to enforce against the assets attached.[50] Failure to comply with this provision will render the original court order a nullity. In any event the order authorising the arrest of the assets has to be executed within three months of the date of the order.[51]

The court which grants the original order retains jurisdiction to deal with any issues arising in relation to the terms of the order rendered. In practice it is common for the Debtor upon service of the order to make an application to the court to either lift or vary the order of arrest. The court will then fix a hearing in the presence of both parties to determine the issues raised. Typically the Debtor may attempt to persuade the court that the claim is not well founded in principle or the amount claimed is excessive. The Debtor may also seek to persuade the court that there is no risk of the claim not being satisfied i.e. because the Debtor is a substantial company etc.

The court upon hearing the parties may either lift vary or maintain the original order for the *Saisie Conservatoire*. A right of appeal lies to the Court of Appeal.

In comparison with the procedural and evidential requirements before an English court the procedure before the French courts is in practice simpler and less expensive. One reason for this is that French procedural law, contrary to the practice of the English judicial system, does not provide for the judge to examine witnesses. Consequently there is no requirement for the Claimant to swear an affidavit now known as a witness statement in support of his application.

The French rules governing the *Saisie Conservatoire* do not strictly require the Claimant to make full and frank disclosure of all material issues to the judge upon pain of the court having the power to discharge the order. But clearly the Claimant creditor must not mislead the court. For example if the Claimant has misrepresented the facts in his petition then the Debtor Defendant could seek an order that the *Saisie Conservatoire* should be withdrawn and ask for damages to be awarded for any loss incurred as a result of the arrest.

Finally, there is no requirement under French law for the Claimant creditor to provide an undertaking in damages to indemnify the Debtor or any third party affected by the arrest if the order should in the future be discharged. But the French court does have the jurisdiction at all times to hear any issues in relation to problems arising in the performance of the *Saisie Conservatoire* and its effect on other parties.[52]

[48] Art. L. 512-2 CPCE.

[49] Art. R522-5 CPCE.

[50] Arts. L.511-4 and R. 511-7 CPCE.

[51] Art. R. 511-6 CPCE.

[52] Art. R. 511-5 CPCE.

Normally the cost of enforcing the order will be for the debtor but the court does have jurisdiction to find the Claimant liable to the debtor for any losses the latter has suffered if the arrest is subsequently lifted.[53] The French courts may ask for counter security to be provided by a party seeking an arrest but this is very rare in practice. The courts will not normally require any counter security to be put up by the Claimant as a condition for obtaining the *Saisie Conservatoire*.

2.7.2 The Procedure for Obtaining a Mareva Injunction or Freezing Order

Today, the High Court[54] in London will normally be the jurisdiction which will have power to grant a Mareva Injunction or Freezing Order. Many applications for Freezing Orders will in practice involve overseas parties active in international commerce with assets held in the UK. This means that, unlike the position in France in relation to the *Saisie Conservatoire*, if an English based creditor has a claim against an English based debtor where there is a serious risk that the claim will not be satisfied through lack of assets the English based creditor will only be able to avail himself of the remedy of the Freezing Order if he can show deliberate attempts by his debtor to dissipate assets.[55]

In practice an urgent application will be made normally by a barrister before a judge in chambers ex parte, that is without notice. The commercial court even during vacation period will have judges available for such urgent applications on duty. The application will be made orally before the judge supported by an affidavit/witness statement sworn either by the solicitor acting for the applicant or an officer of the clients setting out the grounds upon which the Freezing Order is sought.[56] The affidavit will include within exhibits the principal documents upon which the application is based. These will be typically the contract, evidence of the risk of dissipation of

---

[53] Art. L. 512-2 CPCE.

[54] Interestingly, while Mareva Injunctions were more frequently applied for in the Commercial Court, "*Freezing Orders are now widespread in all Divisions and sub-divisions of the High Court*." Quoted from Hoyle 2006, para 4.5., at 33. Note as well that as per the High Court and County Courts Jurisdiction (Amendment) Order 1995 nominated specialist judges of the Central London County Court Business List can also hear Freezing Order applications though only in cases worth up to £200,000. *Id.* section 3.13., at 23.

[55] Hoyle distinguishes two standards. If the evidence shows that the debt "*will not be paid because the defendant is so arranging his affairs, [rather than that only] it might not be paid because the defendant could so arrange his affairs,*" normally it may be hard to obtain a Freezing Order in the second situation. See Hoyle, para 4.25, at 37. Consequently, there must be evidence that the defendant is "*either disposing of assets in such a manner that the only inference to be drawn is that he is making himself judgment-proof, or it must be shown that he is living or trading in a manner so different from his general pattern or from normal explicable practice that the only in reference to be drawn is that he is deliberately creating a state of affairs where he cannot meet any likely judgment debt.*" *Id.* para 4.24., at 37.

[56] See also Hoyle (2006), para 4.7., at 33.

assets, arguments in support of the grounds for a good arguable case as well as full and frank disclosure of all material issues.[57] If satisfied that the application is justified the judge will normally grant the order[58] which will be served immediately by the solicitors on the Defendant and third parties which may hold the assets.[59] Thereafter the Defendant or any third party once served with the Freezing Order may make an application before the judge to lift or vary the order or raise any issues affecting the order. Such an application would be served on the Claimant and the Judge would then fix an urgent hearing date for the two parties to be heard.

The application to the High Court judge will usually be made ex parte i.e. without notice to the Debtor. It is a requirement for the lawyers making the application to produce an affidavit from the officers of the client or perhaps their solicitor in support of the evidence of the claim.[60] The Judge will have to be persuaded that:

- Firstly, there is a good arguable case for the claim in question;
- Secondly, there is a serious risk that assets will be dissipated or removed from the jurisdiction to frustrate satisfaction of the claim;
- Thirdly, the Claimant or his lawyer will have to confirm that they have made full and frank disclosure to the court of all material issues;
- Fourthly, the Claimant will have to give an undertaking in appropriate terms as to damages to indemnify the Defendant or any third party which may suffer losses if the Freezing Order is discharged or for any losses which may be incurred by the third party in the performance of the injunction, and

Finally, as the court is exercising a discretion the judge must satisfy himself that it would be just and convenient in all the circumstances to grant the order.

If the court grants the application then the lawyers for the Claimant will be given an appropriate order by the court and will then have to communicate the terms of the Order to the Defendant and any third parties affected by it. Third parties may

---

[57]As further clarified by Lord Denning MR in *Third Chandris Shipping Corporation v Unimarine SA*, [1979] QB 645; [1979] Lloyd's Rep. 184, CA, enclosing to the affidavit "*sufficient exhibits to the affidavit to underline a particular point, especially in relation to credit-worthiness or the usual course of dealings, are vital*." Hoyle 2006, para 1.13., at 5.

[58]This is in particular due to the fact that the claimant "*does not need to have a strong prima facie case, nor one which will succeed in summary proceedings. Rather, the test is whether he has a good arguable claim, coupled with the court's discretion in any particular case*." See Hoyle 2006, para 4.20, at 36. For what a 'good arguable claim' is sources point to the case *Ninemia Maritime Corporation v. Trave Schiffahrts GmbH & Co. KG (The Niedersachsen)* [1983] 1 WLR 1412; [1983] 2 Lloyd's Rep. 600, CA, which stated: "*A 'good arguable case' is no doubt the minimum which the plaintiff must show in order to cross what the judge rightly described as the 'threshold' for the exercise of the jurisdiction. But at the end of the day court must consider the evidence as a whole in deciding whether or not to exercise this statutory jurisdiction*." Quoted by Hoyle 2006, para 4.20, at 36.

[59]Id. sections 4.9, 4.10, and 4.11, at 34. The notice can first be faxed or scanned and emailed to the person(s) holding the defendant's assets as soon as possible. It is advisable to get a clean draft sealed by the court soon after the hearing, "*[a] copy [of which] should be sent on later and the original must be served according to the terms of the order*."

[60]Civil Procedure Rules, PD 25A, par 3.1.

be given notice of the Order or it may be served upon them. This communication can be by most effective means (personal service, post or leaving the order at a specified place) as far as English defendants are concerned (or by fax and email if the defendant agrees to this).[61] As regards foreign domiciled defendants service can be conducted in accordance with international treaties on the subject, via local government authorities or British consular authorities or by any method permitted by local rules,[62] but alternative methods can also be authorised by the courts.[63] Service by a court bailiff is not essential in England.

When the Order of the court is served on the Defendant and any third parties it is important to note that the effect of the service of the Order is not to attach the assets involved in the strict sense that the assets will no longer be available to the Debtor. Rather, the Order will give "only" a notice to the Defendant and or any third party that failure to respect the court Order would be a contempt of court exposing the Defendant or third party to proceedings including penal sanctions for contempt of court.[64] In this respect it important to understand that the Mareva Injunction is an action in personam and not in rem. English procedural law, unlike French law, recognises actions in personam i.e. against a person and actions in rem (i.e. against a chattel or asset). For example the jurisdiction of the English Admiralty Court has for centuries allowed a vessel to be arrested by an action in rem against the vessel. However the Mareva Injunction is not an action in rem attaching the assets concerned but an action in personam against the debtor Defendant. The consequences of the Defendant failing to comply with the Order served will be exposure to contempt proceedings which could include penal sanctions.

2.8 On the Role of Contempt of Court Rules

Throughout this monograph it has been pointed out that from its origins the Mareva Injunction or Freezing Order was an order made in personam directing a party not to do certain things and usually not to dispose of its assets. Consequently it was accepted that the assets themselves which are the subject of the order are not arrested or attached as such. If the Defendant or third party which may hold the assets in question has been served with the order failure to obey its terms will expose them to penal sanctions because such a failure could be characterized as a contempt of court. Therefore in practice if a party amenable to the jurisdiction of the English courts is served with a Freezing Order it will clearly be conscious that refusing to comply with

---

[61] Civil Procedure Rules Part 6.20 *et seq.*

[62] Civil Procedure Rules Part 6.40, but specific rules apply to overseas companies registered in the UK (see Companies Act 2006, section 1139).

[63] Civil Procedure Rules Part 6.15.

[64] See in particular the UK Contempt of Courts Act 1981. Willful violation of UK contempt of court laws could lead to imprisonment, fine or sequestration of assets. The existence of a distinct contempt of court law is the reflection of the philosophy that "*disobedience of a court order, even in a 'private matter' is a public wrong*." Bell et al., French Law 2008, at 116.

the order could have severe consequences if the party is held as a result of such failure to have committed a contempt of court. In practice when such Freezing Orders are served they can be endorsed with a penal notice pointing out the consequences of a failure to obey comply with the injunction.

Reported cases dealing with the consequences of committing a contempt of court are relatively scarce. There is a detailed discussion of the issues involved in considering whether there has been a contempt of court in the case of *Z Bank v D1 and others* [1994].[65] The Court stressed that the English courts had long been recognized to have an inherent jurisdiction to enforce their own orders which included powers to punish those, whether natural persons or corporations, who disobey the orders of the court.[66] In that case the Court held that the Defendants and their bank had committed serious contempt of court in their failure to comply with the Freezing Orders served. The Court therefore ordered the sequestration of the assets of the bank as a consequence to compel compliance with the injunctions served. Criminal contempt proceedings, although rare, exist as well. For example, in *Pospischil v. Phillips*[67] the contemnor was first sentenced to imprisonment for ten weeks that was reduced to six weeks on appeal.[68] A non-party can also be held to have acted in contempt of court, however, only if "*1/he knows of the injunction and 2/he knowingly aided and abetted breach of it, or he knowingly acted contrary to its purpose.*"[69]

However the position as to the effective enforceability of a *Saisie Conservatoire* is quite different. The effect of a *Saisie Conservatoire* is to render the assets in question unavailable to the debtor or any third party like a bank holding the assets. The order authorizing the arrest is served on the debtor or third party holding the assets by a court bailiff. If the order is subsequently lifted or varied then this too will require service by a court bailiff upon the debtor or third party to release or vary the order. Consequently the French procedural rules concerning contempt of court ("*Refus d'obtemperer a une ordonnance de justice*") do not play an important role in the enforcement of a *Saisie Conservatoire* unlike the position resulting from a court granting a Freezing Order in England.

---

[65] *Z Bank v D1 and others* (1994) 1 LLR 656 (and particularly at 659, 660).

[66] As Glidewell LJ expressed on the function of the contempt in the context of Mareva Injunctions in the case *Pospischil v. Phillips* [1988 CAT 0031]—"*But the plaintiff is not the only interested party. The public is an interested party, because it is and it should be known that it is of the highest importance that orders as serious as Mareva injunctions made by the court are there to be observed and not flouted.*" Quoted by Hoyle 2006, para 9.35, at 157.

[67] *Pospischil v. Philllips*, 1988 CAT 0031. In this case, the Mareva Injunction was issued because the plaintiff's solicitors discovered that the defendant intended to sell certain real property (immovable), already encumbered by more charges, and located in Nottinghamshire. The defendant was prohibited from 'selling, charging or otherwise dealing with the property' save with the prior written consent of the plaintiff's solicitors. Irrespective of that, the defendant sold the property without informing the solicitors and immediately spent the received purchase price. He did not inform his own solicitor—who sold the asset for him—of the Mareva either. The court found that this was a serious and deliberate breach of the Mareva Injunction.

[68] Hoyle (2006), para 9.35, at 157.

[69] Gee S.Q.C. (2016), para 21-006, at 734.

The court has a discretion as to what sanctions may be imposed upon a Defendant who has wilfully refused to comply with an order which may include an order disbarring the Defendant from defending the substantive proceedings brought in support of the Freezing Order. It should also be noted here that depending on the order made some or all of the assets affected by the Freezing Order may not necessarily be located within the jurisdiction of the English court.[70] The effective means of enforcement of the injunction will in such cases rely on the amenability of the Defendant to be pursued with proceedings for contempt of court before the English court in the event that the Defendant fails to comply with the order.

A further point which should be observed in relation to the orders made by the courts is that the Judge will be invited to make provision in the Order for all relevant circumstances which could affect the Defendant or any third party in complying with the Order. This means in practice that the court may, upon an application to the court, allow for the Defendant to have the right to continue to make certain payments from the assets or funds attached in order to continue the business activities of his company. In this respect the assets in question are not immobilised as in the case of a *Saisie Conservatoire*. Such orders are commonly referred to as *Angel Bell orders* following the name of the case in question.[71]

In practice when an order is served upon a Defendant then it will be common for the parties to seek a hearing before the court to hear issues arising from the granting of the application. Typically the Defendant may seek to lift or vary the Order while the Claimant will resist such an application. Appeals will lie from the decision of the court to the Court of Appeal.

[70]See, e.g., *Hamlin v. Hamlin* [1985] 2 All ER 1037; [1986] 1 FLR 61, CA. In this case, the wife—after divorce—asked the Court of Appeal to freeze certain property of the former husband located in Spain. This property was the only unencumbered property he could sell off to pay his outstanding debts. The wife asked a Freezing Order based on the Matrimonial Causes Act 1973 and while the first instance court refused to grant the Order for lack of jurisdiction, on appeal the decision was overturned. This because "*the jurisdiction of the courts was specifically to be exercised in personam against persons who were amenable to the court's coercive powers to enforce orders made against them*," but also because the law's application is not restricted to property situated in England and Wales. See Hoyle (2006), para 8.33, at 125.

[71]*Angel Bell* [1981] QB 65. The case involved a ship named 'Angel Bell,' the shorthand reference stems herefrom. In the case, the ship sank and the plaintiffs claimed damages for the lost cargo from the Panamian shipowner and obtained a Mareva Injunction prohibiting the defendant from dealing with and removing assets of the defendant out of the jurisdiction. The creditors of the defendant have, however, intervened as the remaining assets of the defendant—proceeds of insurance policies held by brokers—were insufficient to pay both the plaintiff and the intervening creditors. The court modified the Mareva Injunction and allowed the repayment of the loan from insurance proceeds because granting the Mareva Injunction "*was not to improve the position of any claimants to the property of an insolvent debtor but rather to prevent injustice*" by prohibiting removal of assets out of the jurisdiction.

2.9 A Comparison of the *Saisie Conservatoire* and the Freezing Order Mareva Injunction as Remedies for a Creditor Seeking to Enforce a Claim

2.9.1 Speed, Simplicity and Cost

Both the *Saisie Conservatoire* and Freezing Order are very common procedural remedies sought before the respective courts of England and France. Such orders can be obtained quickly and effectively. The legal costs involved in obtaining a Mareva Injunction Freezing Order will normally be higher as a consequence of the requirement of English procedure that witness evidence be put in support of such applications. But English procedural rules unlike French rules allow a successful party to obtain a substantial indemnity for legal costs incurred from an opponent in the event of success. This is because the English legal system allows successful litigants to obtain costs orders against their opponents. This practice is not a feature of the French civil law system where the judges have a discretion to award costs against unsuccessful parties.[72] Such costs orders will often be lump sum figures which will quite frequently be inadequate to indemnify the successful party for the costs actually incurred.

2.9.2 The Consequences of Obtaining a Saisie Conservatoire *and Freezing Order and the Effect of the Order*

In the case of the *Saisie Conservatoire* the assets in question are attached and are no longer available to the Debtor. The assets are therefore arrested and the existence of the arrest may give the Creditor certain preferential rights over the assets attached in comparison with other creditors.

The Freezing Order is not an attachment or arrest of the assets concerned like an action in rem but an injunction in personam restraining the Debtor from removing or dissipating the assets. Consequently no property rights are conferred upon the Creditor as a result of the granting of a Freezing Order.

A further consequence of this distinction is that the assets of the Debtor are not arrested and immobilised as they would be pursuant to a civil law *Saisie Conservatoire*. If the Debtor or a third party like a bank breaches the court Order then they will be exposed to an action for contempt of court. But interesting legal questions arise when the breach of the court Order is innocent i.e. not deliberate. In a recent case[73] involving a Claimant obtaining a Freezing Order a bank, innocently due to

[72] Article 700 of the French Code of Civil Procedure allows a court to award costs incurred by a successful litigant to be paid by the debtor. But in practice the courts award lump sums which will not necessarily correspond to the real legal costs incurred.

[73] *Commissioners of Customs and Excise v Barclays Bank* (2006) 2 LLR 327.

an omission to have a proper system in place to prevent payments from the accounts concerned, allowed money which should have been blocked by the Freezing Order to be paid out of the account. It was accepted by the parties that the omission was innocent. The Claimant brought an action in negligence against the Bank for failing to have a proper system in place to insure that the Freezing Order would be respected for the accounts. The case was disputed by the Bank which succeeded on appeal to the House of Lords in reversing the decision of the Court of Appeal holding it liable. The House of Lords decided that a third party bank served with a Freezing Order did not owe a duty of care to a Claimant to put in place a proper system to ensure that payments were not made from accounts affected by the Order. A similar situation would not normally arise in the case of a *Saisie Conservatoire* because the bank account in question would be arrested i.e. attached pursuant to the service on the bank of the order by a court bailiff.

2.9.3 Counter Security or Undertakings in Damages

The Creditor seeking a *Saisie Conservatoire* will not normally be required to provide counter security to the Debtor. The Claimant seeking a Freezing Order should always be required to give an undertaking to the court often to be fortified by a bank guarantee to cover the risk that the granting of the Freezing Order causes losses to the Debtor or third party.

2.9.4 Ancillary Orders Which Can Be Granted by the Courts to Assist Enforcement of Provisional Measures

A French court granting *a Saisie Conservatoire* can only make an order to attach assets located within the jurisdiction of the court. If the Claimant does not have complete knowledge of the location of the Debtor's assets within or outside French jurisdiction the court can offer no assistance here.[74]

As opposed to France, the High Court in England granting a Freezing Order has over the last few years extended its powers to give very considerable assistance to an unpaid creditor to seek information from his debtor as to the location of his assets within or outside the jurisdiction including injunctions to restrain the debtor from dissipating his worldwide assets. This is far from being an unimportant distinguishing feature of English law. In fact, the efficiency of the Freezing Orders to a great extent is due also to the ancillary orders developed parallel with the Mareva Injunction. As

[74]As one of the few English language articles on the *Saisie Conservatoire* suggested commenting on the way this provisional measure works in practice when attachment of receivables is sought, "*[t]he only practical difficulty in this regard is properly identifying the relevant third parties*." Lowe and Jaeger (1993), at 256.

one renowned source correctly noted: "*A skilful choice of ancillary orders makes both Search*[75] *and Freezing Orders even more powerful weapons in a claimant's armoury.*"[76] In fact, English courts are even willing to grant orders that allow for search in a foreign jurisdictions.[77] Today, the Search Orders are based on the Civil Procedure Act 1997.

2.10 Jurisdiction, Recognition and Enforceability of Freezing Orders in EU Member States—Potential Conflicts and Uncertainties

2.10.1 General Considerations

Until we see the exact results of Brexit[78] and in particular how it will affect the issue of the recognition and enforcement of provisional measures made in other member states, we should continue to base our views on the principle that both France and the United Kingdom are members of the European Union. At the moment, therefore EU Regulation 44/2001 ("the Regulation") replaced by EU Regulation 1215/2014 is the relevant piece of legislation that sets out the European Union's rules as to mutual recognition and enforcement of judgments.[79] But the Regulation deals mostly with the recognition of judgments in relation to substantive proceedings on the merits. The

---

[75]The Search Order was formerly known as the Anto Piller order after the case *Anton Piller KG v. Manufacturing Processes Ltd.* [1976] 1 Ch 55, CA (8 December 1975). The Search Order's function is to "*to ensure that evidence in the defendant's possession is not destroyed or disposed of so as to make it difficult, if not impossible, to prove his case.*" It is also issued *ex parte* and allows "*the claimant's solicitor to inspect documents and chattels on the defendant's premises, and to take photographs of the originals or copies of them.*" See Hoyle (2006), para 8.2., at 115.

[76]Hoyle (2006), para 8.1., at 115.

[77]In the case *Cook Industries Inc. V Galliher* [1979] Ch 439; [1978] 3 WLR 637 the plaintiff (an American corporation) obtained an *ex parte* injunction restraining the friend of the defendant to dispose of or remove any contents of a flat located in Paris. The court also ordered the French friend to allow a French attorney (who was also an English barrister) to inspect the flat in Paris.

[78]Pursuant to two working papers published by the UK Government at the date of writing this monograph the position adopted by the UK is essentially that the existing framework under pre Brexit agreements (ie the Lugano Convention, EU Regulation 44/2001 and EU Regulation 1215/2012) should form the basis for recognition and enforcement of EU and UK court decisions in future. But the role of the CJEU in relation to disputes between the EU and the UK is quite uncertain as the UK Government is suggesting that the CJEU should not have jurisdiction to determine such disputes because it is not a neutral court. See the working paper entitled *Providing a Cross-Border Civil Judicial Cooperation Framework—A Future Partnership Paper* is available at: <https://www.gov.uk/government/uploads/system/uploads/attachment_data/file/639271/Providing_a_cross-border_civil_judicial_cooperation_framework.pdf>. [Accessed 15 Apr. 2018].

[79]The Brussels Convention 1968, which was largely superseded by this Regulation, is still applicable in certain limited instances, notably involving territories of Member States to which the Regulation does not apply.

provisions of the Regulation in relation to jurisdiction for substantive proceedings replace the rules of the Member States existing before then.

The basic principle put forward by the Regulation is that the court of the principal place of business of the Defendant will have jurisdiction. The Regulation deals only very briefly with the jurisdiction of the EU Member courts in connection with interim measures like arrests. Article 31 of Regulation 44/2001 and Article 35 of Regulation 1215/2014 which replaced it provide that the EU Member courts can continue to grant ancillary relief and interim orders in accordance with their own national rules and this power is extended to arrest of assets in support of substantive legal proceedings to be brought before the courts of another Member State. The Regulations therefore refer each Member State court to its own national rules in respect of such provisional protective orders. If an arrest of goods has been ordered in one Member State in accordance with its own rules then it should normally be enforceable in other Member States.

It should be noted that the discussion which follows is restricted to the situation where the English and French courts are being invited to provide provisional orders in support of substantive proceedings to be commenced before other Member State courts. The powers of the French and English courts to give interim orders and ancillary relief solely in relation to proceedings to be commenced before their own courts is outside of the scope of the discussion which follows. It is to be noted in this respect that the French courts may have wider powers to order interim relief including orders against French based debtors when substantive proceedings are commenced against them in France than their powers to authorise arrest orders or interim relief when the substantive proceedings are to be commenced before another EU Member court and the assets involved are not within the French jurisdiction.

2.10.2 Jurisdiction-Related Issues

The French and English legal systems outside of the Regulations have quite different rules as to the jurisdiction of their courts to deal with substantive proceedings. In France, article 14 of the Civil Code confers jurisdiction on French courts over foreign nationals by reason of the French nationality of a Claimant involved in the dispute.[80] By contrast in England common law rules will apply, and various factors will be considered before a court accepts jurisdiction (nationality/domicile of the parties, place of performance/breach of an obligation, presence of related proceedings, convenience).

As to jurisdiction to arrest assets the French courts do not require the presence of the debtor within its territory to justify an arrest. In this case, it is sufficient that the assets to be attached are located in France because the court where the interim arrest

[80] Article 14 of the Code Civil provides that a foreign party non-resident in France can be sued before the French courts in relation to obligations contractually undertaken in favour of a French citizen. The article is of course inapplicable to EU member states as a result of the Brussels Convention.

order is to be carried out will have jurisdiction.[81] The approach of the English courts is rather that the debtor should have some presence in the English jurisdiction in order to justify the involvement of the English courts. The case law reveals that it is not necessarily essential that the debtor should be resident or domiciled in England but the court should have in personam jurisdiction over the defendant.[82] In some cases a sufficient link between the jurisdiction of the English court and the debtor may be established if the debtor is '*amenable*' to the jurisdiction of the English courts. This could be satisfied for example if the debtor has business activities connected with England and in the case of physical persons like directors needs to visit the UK regularly.[83]

There is little guidance in article 31 of EU Regulation 44/2001 and Article 35 of Regulation 1215/2014 (which replaced the former) on the circumstances which allow a Member court to have jurisdiction to grant interlocutory orders in relation to substantive proceedings before the courts of another Member State. The issue was considered in an important decision of the ECJ, in the *Van Uden* case in 1998,[84] where the ECJ indicated that a Member court granting interim orders under article 31 of the Regulation needed to be satisfied that there was a real connecting link between the subject matter of the measures sought and the territorial jurisdiction of the contracting state before which such measures are sought.

The facts of the case were briefly as follows. An application was made by a Claimant before the court in Rotterdam against a German Defendant to obtain an advance payment from the court in relation to a contract subject to arbitration in Holland. The ECJ considered that the application in question was not covered by article 31 of the Regulation. The remedy was not in the nature of an order to suspend or preserve rights as required by the Regulation. Moreover the ECJ considered that the order sought was inappropriate because it would necessarily interfere with the jurisdiction of the court which would determine the merits of the dispute if the interlocutory judge made an order granting a partial payment to be made to the Claimant. The ECJ however insisted that the Member court granting a conservative arrest of assets which would fall within the terms of article 31 of the Regulation must satisfy itself that there is a "real connection" between the measure sought and territorial jurisdiction of the court in question. It was suggested that for example the fact that a debtor may have a bank account in one Member State may not be enough to justify the court in that State to grant interlocutory orders in respect of any assets held there if there is no other connection with the debtor and that State.

---

[81] Art. R. 121-2 CPCE.

[82] See for example *Royal Bank of Scotland v Fal Oil Co Ltd and others at* (2013) 1 Lloyds Law Reporter 327 for the circumstances in which the Court may consider it appropriate to make in personam orders against parties who may not be normally resident in the jurisdiction but will have a sufficient connection to make the orders enforceable.

[83] *Royal Bank of Scotland v Fail Oil Co Ltd.* (2013)1 Lloyds Law Reporter 327 at 339 par 46.

[84] *Van Uden Maritime BV v Deco Line* Case 391/95 (1998) 1 ECR 7091.

2.10.3 Recognition and Enforcement of Mareva Injunction Freezing Order by Member States of the European Union

There is a recent decision of the European Court of Justice which has approved of recognition and enforcement of an English Mareva Injunction Freezing Order pursuant to the terms of EU Regulation 44/2001. In the case of *Rudolf Meroni v Recoletos Limited*[85] there was a reference to the ECJ by the Supreme Court of Latvia involving recognition of an English Freezing Order. The recognition of the English Freezing Order was challenged before the Latvian courts by a third party affected by the order on the grounds that it was contrary to public policy. The Freezing Order issued by the High Court in the UK ordered the Defendant to refrain from disposing of his assets including shares in a company incorporated in Latvia. The application to contest the order was made by a third party affected by the order who was the representative and manager of the property frozen. The objection was based on the argument that the third party had not been heard by the High Court in the UK and therefore that constituted a breach of public policy under Article 34 of EU Regulation 44/2001. The ECJ dismissed the objection on the grounds that matters alleging breach of public policy had to be interpreted strictly and it was clear that the third party served with the Freezing Order was entitled to contest it before the High Court. The dispute did not however involve recognition of a worldwide Freezing Order, which we will take a brief look at next.

2.10.4 Worldwide Freezing Orders Before French Courts and the European Court of Justice

The nature of this real connection has since given rise to considerable discussion and doubt in English legal circles as to whether the ECJ would disapprove of the practice of the English courts to grant worldwide freezing orders relating to assets outside of the jurisdiction of the English court. In relation to French practice and academic opinion it would seem quite uncontroversial that a French interlocutory judge exercising powers under article 31 of the former Regulation 44/2001 and Article 35 of the new Regulation 1215/2014 would not have jurisdiction to grant an arrest of assets situated outside of France.[86]

[85] Judgment of the Court of First Chamber as of 25th of May 2016 in Case C-559/14.

[86] No such powers are conferred by national legislation on interim arrest orders i.e. the CPCE.

However, the issue of whether a worldwide Freezing Order could be enforced by a French court within the terms of article 31 of the Regulation 44/2001 has been considered by the French Supreme Court. In the case of *Stolzenberg v Sote Daimler Chrysler Canada*[87] the *Cour de Cassation* held that a Mareva Injunction granted in England restraining a Defendant from disposing of his assets worldwide was enforceable under the terms of article 31 of the Regulation. In particular the *Cour de Cassation* observed that there was, contrary to the allegation made before the court, no breach of international comity or the principles of the EU in allowing such an injunction to be enforced. The *Cour de Cassation* considered that the essential feature of a Freezing Order was, in contrast to a *Saisie Conservatoire*, that it was an order restraining the defendant from doing certain things i.e. disposing of assets. It was quite clear that the effect of the Freezing Order was not to attach assets as such or have any consequences in terms of property rights over the assets of the Defendant. The *Cour de Cassation* concluded that in this respect unlike the English anti-suit injunctions which had been sanctioned (i.e. determined unlawful by the ECJ) there was no reason of public international order to justify refusal of recognition of such an injunction. The decision of the *Cour de Cassation* has met with approval from English and French legal commentators.[88]

Although the French Supreme Court has decided that a worldwide Mareva Injunction can be enforced in France, it is not clear that the reasoning of the *Cour de Cassation* decision will be followed by the ECJ if the matter comes before that court. Given the position taken by the ECJ in relation to the validity of anti-suit injunctions as a matter of European law and practice it could possibly take a fundamentally different view from the French *Cour de Cassation.* For example the reasoning of the *Cour de Cassation* in the above decision is very similar to the views put forward by Lord Hobhouse in the House of Lords in *Turner v Grovit*.[89] Lord Hobhouse defended the jurisdiction of the English courts to grant anti-suit injunctions on the grounds that the anti-suit injunction was not based on "*any pretension to the exercise of judicial ... rights abroad*" but solely upon the fact that the party being restrained is subject to the in personam jurisdiction of the English court. Lord Hobhouse went on to observe that the terminology of anti-suit injunctions is misleading because the order granted by an English court is not directed against the foreign court but only in personam to the party before it.[90] But this reasoning was certainly not followed by the ECJ in its decision in *Turner v Grovit*.[91]

---

[87] Cass 1ère Civil, 30 June 2004 JCP G 2004 11 10198.

[88] See new footnote adding article of Nicolas Bouche Recueil Dalloz 2004 p. 2743 for an interesting discussion of the decision of the French Supreme Court to Footnote 54.

[89] (2001) UKHL 65, (2002) 1 WLR 107 (22)–(29).

[90] Id at (23).

[91] Case C-159/02 (2004) 2 LLR 169.

The issue of whether a worldwide Mareva Injunction can be enforced in an EU member state without doing violence to any fundamental principles of EU law has not yet come before the ECJ. The new text of the original EU Regulation 44/2001 offers little guidance on the question of enforceability of provisional measures in EU member states. Regulation No 1215/2012 similarly to its predecessor Regulation 44/2001 simply states at Article 35 that the courts of a member state may order provisional and protective measures available under the law of that EU state even if the courts of another EU Member State have jurisdiction as to the substance of the matter. The new Regulation 1215/2012 does have materially different provisions in its preamble relating to arbitration which have been interpreted generally to give support to the view that the controversial decision of the ECJ in the *Front Comor* case[92] refusing to enforce English anti suit injunctions in relation to a breach of an arbitration clause could be reversed by a future decision.

In this respect the much awaited decision of the ECJ in the *Gazprom matter*[93] offers little guidance from the decision itself. The ECJ held that an arbitration decision which issued an anti-suit order to deter a party from acting in breach of an arbitration agreement was enforceable as a matter of the internal and international law of the EU Member state. But in the Gazprom case it is interesting to note that the Advocate General Wathelet submitted to the Court that in the light of the amended new EU Regulation 1215/2012 the decision of the ECJ in the *Front Comor* case should be reversed as arbitration and accessory orders related to arbitration are clearly excluded from the ambit of the Regulation. But this will not be of direct relevance to the issue of whether a worldwide Mareva Injunction should be capable of enforcement in the EU.

As stated above the decision of the *Cour de Cassation* does not deal exhaustively with all the issues arising out of enforcement and recognition of Freezing Orders outside of England. For example it is common practice for orders drafted by the English courts in such cases to include provisions dealing with the effect of the Freezing Orders on third parties like foreign banks. Such orders have standard provisions stating that the third party abroad will not be prevented from complying with orders of its own courts in relation to the assets. But such a provision is in itself an example of a potential interference with the jurisdiction of the court outside England. As has been pointed out earlier recent decisions of the English courts in this field have embarked upon consideration of the factors which should be taken into account by the English court when deciding whether to grant a worldwide freezing order in relation to proceedings abroad.[94] Such discussions include consideration of whether the foreign court would have similar powers to grant such orders and if not why. These issues again could be perceived to involve potential interference of the English court into the practices of a foreign court which the ECJ may regard as incompatible with the

[92] *Front Comor West Tankers Inc v Allianz SPA* (C-185/07).

[93] *Gazprom OAO v. Republic of Lithuania* (Case C-536/13) dated 13 May 2015.

[94] See *Credit Suisse Fides Trust SA v Cuoghi* (1998) 1 QB 818, *Motorola Credit Corporation v Uzan* (No 2) (2004) 1 WLR 113, *Dadourian Group Int Inc v Simms* (2006) 2 LLR 354, *Royal Bank of Scotland PLC v Fal Oil Co Ltd.* (2013) 1 Lloyds Law Reporter 327.

principles of the EU rules on the respect to be given by the courts of Member States to other Member State courts.

In relation to the jurisdiction of the English court to grant worldwide freezing orders restraining a party amenable to the in personam jurisdiction of the English court several difficulties could arise if this power were to be challenged before the ECJ. Firstly and perhaps most fundamentally the ECJ could consider that in a situation where the assets of the person restrained were outside of the jurisdiction of the English court then there would not be a sufficient real connecting link allowing the court to make such an order. This was suggested by the ECJ in its decision in *Van Uden*.[95] In the earlier decision of the ECJ often cited in this respect the *Denilaur case*[96] it was suggested that the court of the place where the assets in question are situated would be best placed to grant such orders.[97] As for the decisions of the English courts to grant worldwide freezing orders in relation to assets overseas and in respect of persons who are not resident or domiciled in the UK but merely have a sufficient connection with the UK to be amenable to the in personam jurisdiction of the court, the ECJ may well take the view that such links are far too tenuous to be considered a real connection with the court for the purposes of the Regulation.

2.11 Conclusions

The current practice of the English courts to grant interim relief including Freezing Orders affecting assets outside of the English jurisdiction in connection with substantive proceedings pursued before another EU Member court has not been fully examined in relation to the rules on recognition of EU Member judgments in Regulation 44/2001 or in the new EU Regulation 1215/2012. The most recent decisions of the English courts seem implicitly to accept that this novel practice may involve the risk of interference with the management of the substantive proceedings by the other EU Member court. There may also be a risk that the other Member court may object on grounds of comity to the English court making orders which may be incompatible with orders of the other court. If the ECJ will adopt a similar approach to such issues as it has taken in connection with the English practice of issuing anti suit injunctions in the Turner v Gromit case then the English courts may again be criticised for adopting legal measures which are implicitly inconsistent with the objectives of the rules of the European Union in relation to recognition and enforcement of judgments. Both the new and the old EU Regulations offer very limited guidance in connection with the jurisdiction of EU Member courts to grant interim orders including attachments of assets.

---

[95]C-391/95.

[96]*Bernard Denilaur v SNC Couchet Freres* (C-125/79).

[97]Id para 16.

And of course a further cause for uncertainty is the decision of the United Kingdom in its referendum of 2016 to leave the European Union. It is impossible at the time of writing this monograph to predict what form the new relationship between the United Kingdom and the European Union will take in connection the enforcement and recognition of judgments. But it would be logical to assume that if the United Kingdom wishes its judgments to be recognized and enforced in the European Union it will have to accept rules along the lines of the amended Brussels and Lugano Conventions as defined in the latest EU Regulation 1215/2012. From a practical perspective one reason why the issue may not have been brought to the attention of the ECJ to date may simply be that it is relatively rare for parties to seek to enforce World Wide Freezing Orders before the courts of other EU Member States.

Similarly ancillary orders which require a Defendant to make a statement disclosing the location of his assets may rarely be enforced before another Member court. It is also not clear whether such ancillary orders would fall within the definition of art 31 of EU Regulation 44/2001 or Article 35 of EU Regulation 1215/2012 as conservative measures arresting assets. For example a measure ordering the hearing of a witness to determine whether a potential claim is well founded is not within article 31 of the Regulation.[98] From a practical perspective it would be more logical for a party who has successfully obtained such orders to seek an order from the court where the assets are located to arrest them rather than make an application to enforce the English Freezing Order or Ancillary Order in respect of those assets.

The English courts normally grant such orders on the basis that the Defendant is amenable to the English jurisdiction and will therefore comply with the order. The sanction involving potential penal measures which could be taken against a Defendant served with a Freezing Order in England resulting from a contempt of court would often be sufficient to deter a party from voluntarily seeking to act in a breach of an injunction. And as has been seen above the effect of the Freezing Order will not be to arrest the assets themselves irrespective of whether the assets are located within or outside the jurisdiction of the English courts. Perhaps in the light of these practical considerations the fear that the ECJ may interfere with the power of the English courts to grant worldwide freezing orders or ancillary orders may be unjustified. And the absence of a reference of this issue to the ECJ for the considerable period of time such orders have been granted by the English courts could be cited as evidence that the concern may not be warranted. Logically in practice parties will rarely seek to enforce an English Freezing Order or ancillary order requiring evidence to be produced of the location of assets before another Member court as opposed to seeking an order for the arrest of the assets themselves located in the other Member State before the court of that State.

---

[98] *St Paul Dairy Industries NV v Unibel Exser BVBA* (2005) ILPr 416.

This monograph has compared the remedies available to unpaid creditors to arrest or attach freeze assets in two major jurisdictions England and France. A comparative study of existing procedural devices in Hungary and Central Europe has also been conducted. As can be seen from the study above, the decisions of the European Court of Justice have not been particularly favourable to some of the remedies exercised by common law English courts which do not have an equivalent in many of the European Union states. The question of the recognition and enforcement of Mareva Injunction Freezing orders involving assets located outside of the UK but in an EU state has not yet been considered by a decision of the ECJ. But earlier decisions of that court in relation to other injunctions notably anti suit injunctions commonly exercised by the English courts have been hostile to such measures on the grounds that they involve interference with the right of EU member courts to determine their own jurisdiction. The United Kingdom decided following the referendum in 2016 that it would leave the EU. The ramifications of that decision in relation to the recognition and enforcement of decisions of the English Courts in the EU have yet to be determined and are beyond the scope of this monograph. It would be logical to assume that the future recognition of English court decisions in the EU would be based on similar provisions as the Brussels and Lugano Conventions of 1968 which are currently in force until the United Kingdom leaves the EU.

English lawyers make no secret of their view that English law and London as a centre for international dispute resolution are very much the jewel in the crown of the United Kingdom. And the Mareva Injunction Freezing Order has been described by leading members of the judiciary as one of the nuclear weapons in their armory.[99] The UK will clearly be very concerned to retain the leading role of English law and London in the resolution of international commercial disputes. But of course the other EU members will naturally be looking for opportunities to take a bigger share of the international legal market with the departure of the UK from the EU. The French *Saisie Conservatoire* is certainly a provisional measure which in terms of speed, cost and efficiency compares very favourably with the Mareva Injunction. Though a recent relatively little know EU regulation on European Account Preservation Orders[100] has opened the way for a cross border right to arrest bank accounts in any EU member state on the basis of a simple procedure. To date there is no evidence that this novel right has been explored by claimants in France. But that may change of course.

[99]Lord Donaldson referred to the tandem of Mareva Injunction and Antol Piller Orders as 'the two nuclear weapons fo the law' in the case *Bank Mellat v. Nikpour (Mohammad Ebrahim)* [1985] FSR 87, CA. This ephitet has been in use ever since beside the *Grupo Mexicano* case by authors of numerous scholarly papers.

[100]Regulation 655/2014 of the European Parliament and of the Council of 15 May 2014 establishing a European Account Prevention Order procedure to facilitate cross-border debt recovery in civil and commercial matters [hereinafter: Regulation 655/2014]. For more detail see the pertaining section below.

References

EU Legislation

Regulation (EU) No 1215/2012 of the European Parliament and of the Council of 12 December 2012 on jurisdiction and the recognition and enforcement of judgments in civil and commercial matters (recast)
Regulation 655/2014 of the European Parliament and of the Council of 15 May 2014 establishing a European Account Prevention Order procedure to facilitate cross-border debt recovery in civil and commercial matters

Domestic Law: France

Code des Procédures Civiles d'Exécution (CPCE) 2012
Law of the 9th July 1991 [JO 14 Juillet p. 9228 and the Decree of the 31st of July 1992 (J0 5 août p.10530)]

Domestic Law: United Kingdom

Civil Jurisdiction and Judgments Act 1982
Contempt of Courts Act 1981
Supreme Court of Judicature (Consolidation) Act 1925 repealed by the Senior Courts Act 1981 (originally named 'the Supreme Court Act 1981')

Domestic Law: United States

Federal Rules of Civil Procedure

Books

Bell J, Boyron S, Whittaker S (2008) Principles of French Law. Oxford University Press, Oxford
Code des Procédures Civiles d'Exécution, Livre Cinquième les Mesures Conservatoires (2013) Edition Dalloz, 104th edn
Davies PS, Virgo G (2013) Equity & Torts: Text, Cases, and Materials. Oxford University Press, Oxford
Gee SQC (2016) Commercial Injunctions, 6th edn. Sweet & Maxwell
Gummow M, Lehane's Equity (2003) Doctrines & Remedies, 4th edn. LexisNexis
Hoyle MSW, Freezing and Search Orders (2006) 4th edn, Informa-London

Articles

Eder B Sir (2013) 30 years before the mast. Lloyd's Marit Commercial Law Q
Gee S (2006) The undertaking in damages. Lloyd's Marit Commercial Law Q
Lowe S, Jaeger J (1993) Protection and enforcement of creditors' rights under French Law. Int Co Commercial Law Rev 4(7):255–258
Merrett L (2008) World wide freezing Orders in Europe. LMCLQ 71
Nicolas Bouche, Recueil Dalloz 2004 p 2743
Sainte RJ (2005) Mise en oeuvre d'une injunction Mareva. La Semaine Juridique, no 6, at 237

Court Cases: European Union

Bernard Denilaur v SNC Couchet Freres (C-125/79)
Gazprom OAO v. Republic of Lithuania (Case C-536/13) dated 13 May 2015
Turner v Gromit Case (C-159/02)
Front Comor West Tankers Inc v Allianz SPA (C-185/07)

Court Cases: United Kingdom

Angel Bell [1981] QB 65
Anton Piller KG v. Manufacturing Processes Ltd [1976] 1 Ch 55, CA (8 December 1975)
Babanaft International Co. S.A v Bahaedine Bassatne and Walid Mohamed Bassatne [1990] Ch 13; [1988] 2 Lloyds Law Reports 435, CA
Bank Mellat v. Nikpour (Mohammad Ebrahim) [1985] FSR 87, CA
Burmester v Burmester (1913)
Cook Industries Inc. V Galliher [1979] Ch 439; [1978] 3 WLR 637
Commissioners of Customs and Excise v Barclays Bank (2006) 2 LLR 327
Credit Suisse Fides Trust SA v Cuoghi (1998) QB 818; [1997] 3 WLR 871, CA
Dadourian Group International Inc. v Simms (2006) Lloyd's Rep. 2 354; EWCA Civ. 399, CA
Energy Ventures Partners Ltd v Malabu Oil & Gas Ltd [2014 EWCA Civ1295]
Hamlin v. Hamlin [1985] 2 All ER 1037; [1986] 1 FLR 61, CA
Lister v Stubbs (1890) 45 Ch.D 1
Lord Justice Scrutton in Jagger v Jagger (1926)
Mareva Compania Naviera SA v International Bulk Carriers SA (the Mareva) (1975) 2 Lloyds Rep. 509 [1980] 1 All ER 213 CA
Motorola Credit Corporation v Uzan [2003] EWCA Civ 752 (2004) 1 WLR 113, CA
Ninemia Maritime Corporation v. Trave Schiffahrts GmbH & Co. KG (The Niedersachsen) [1983] 1 WLR 1412; [1983] 2 Lloyd's Rep. 600, CA
Nippon Yusen Kaisha v Karageorgis (1975) 2 Lloyd's Law Reports 137
Pospischil v. Phillips, 1988 CAT 0031
Rasu Maritima SA v Pertamina (1977) 2 Lloyd's Rep. 397, CA
Republic of Haiti v Duvalier (1989) 1 LLR 111
Royal Bank of Scotland v FAL Oil Co Ltd [2012] 1 Lloyds Law Reports 327
Siskina, The Owners of Cargo Lately Laden on Board the Siskina v. Distos Compania Naviera SA [1979] AC 210; (1978) 1 Lloyds Law Reports
St Paul Dairy Industries NV v Unibel Exser BVBA (2005) ILPr 416

Third Chandris Shipping Corporation v Unimarine SA, [1979] QB 645; [1979] Lloyd's Rep. 184, CA
Van Uden Maritime BV v Deco Line Case 391/95 (1998) 1 ECR 7091
Z Bank v D1 and others (1994) 1 LLR 656

Internet Sources

UK Government, Providing a Cross-Border Civil Judicial Cooperation Framework—A Future Partnership Paper is available at: https://www.gov.uk/government/uploads/system/uploads/attachment_data/file/639271/Providing_a_cross-border_civil_judicial_cooperation_framework.pdf

Chapter 3
Provisional Measures in the United States

Notwithstanding their common origins, English and US law on provisional measures are different today and they may be conceived as two developed yet distinct contemporary regulatory models. Consequently, it is worthwhile to juxtapose the two not only for this reason but also because of the discourse that has been ongoing in the US ever since Justice Scalia formulating the majority opinion rejected the introduction of the American version of English Mareva Injunction into the US legal system in the famous *Grupo Mexicano* case in 1999.[1]

The debate,[2] reawakening with differing intensity from time to time, seems to have revolved around two interrelated key issues: on the one hand, whether the arsenal of preliminary (provisional) remedies US law possesses adequately satisfies the needs of modern commerce as opposed to the "age of slow-moving capital,"[3] and on the other hand, whether introduction of the US variant of Mareva Injunction into US legal system is needed? While the holding of *Grupo Mexicano* still stands,[4] as we will see, the law is far from being stagnant in this area most presumably driving development towards eventual integration of a Mareva-type freezing order into American law. Attempts to bypass *Grupo Mexicano* through using State practices in federal court is not something unknown either,[5] though perhaps it is more typical is to see cases

[1] *Grupo Mexicano de DeSarollo, S.A. v. Alliance Bond Fund, Inc.* 527 U.S. 308 (1999).

[2] Mentioning of few titles should be sufficient to illustrate the dimensions and nature of the US debate. See, e.g., Capper (2005), DiSarro (2011), Wasserman (April, 1992), Barrack et al. (June, 2011), and Goldman (May, 2005).

[3] *Id.* The quite expressive phrase used in the case is: "*the bygone age of slow-moving capital and comparatively immobile wealth.*"

[4] See, e.g., DiSarro (2011).

[5] Hoyle (2006), at 212.

T. Tajti and P. Iglikowski, *A Cross Border Study of Freezing Orders and Provisional Measures*, SpringerBriefs in Law, https://doi.org/10.1007/978-3-319-94349-7_3

where the facts suggest that there may be a need for a more far-reaching version of preliminary injunctions.[6]

3.1 A Brief History of US Law on Provisional Measures

In the history of US law on provisional measures, three landmark signs should be commented upon: partition with English law, the impact of the 1938 Federal Rules of Civil Procedure and the 1999 *Grupo Mexicano* decision of the US Supreme Court. These seem to have generated changes of such intensity in this specific domain of law that allows us to differentiate and talk of the resulting four phases. Unlike English law, however, US law of provisional measures was much more stable throughout this long period. Although some of the remedies have disappeared from use, no such revolutionary invention surfaced as of yet that could not be dwarfed by the Mareva Injunction in England.

As far as the beginnings are concerned, English and US civil procedure law had become significantly different already in the 19th century,[7] though some resemblances have survived up until today. For example, as it has already been mentioned, while English law does not know an interim measure with in rem effects, the American prejudgment attachments create such inchoate liens that are at the same time of priorities that apply both within and outside bankruptcy law. Today, however, one could safely presume that the two laws are radically different. In fact, certain aspects of US law on provisional measures are closer to French or some other civil laws.

From the surviving similarities, in the context of US law one ought to comment primarily on the continued relevance of the division between 'law and equity,'[8]

[6]See, e.g., Barrack et al. (June, 2011). (Commenting on the actions of Irvin Picard, the trustee for the liquidation of Barnard L. Madoff Investment Securities LLC, who asked for several TROs and preliminary injunctions, including prohibiting the defendants "*transferring or otherwise using any known assets*."

[7]As Grant Gilmore, the doyen of US commercial law put it, "*[t]he Revolutionary trauma had instilled in many, perhaps in most, Americans, a hatred of England and all its ways [...]. [The consequent] Anglophobia led [in some States even] to statutes which prohibited the use of English legal materials in court proceedings*." The New Jersey statute (enacted in 1799 and repealed in 1819), for example, forbade use of "*any [English] compilation, commentary, digest, lecture, treatise, or other explanation or exposition of the common law [...]*." Gilmore (1977), at 22. In Gilmore's opinion, this detachment from English law lasting for about two decades was sufficient for development of indigenous American law that was sufficient to start development of distinct law though again increasingly taking a look at developments in England. *Id.* at 23.

[8]The readers not adversed in US nomenclature should bear in mind that the term 'common law' in US legal terminology has three distinct meanings and in figuring out which meaning is being used the context in which they are used is crucial. First, it may be a reference to the Anglo-Saxon system as opposed to civil laws or Islamic law. Secondly, it may denote case law (precedents). Thirdly, in a historical context it is a reference to that branch of law that is not 'equity.' This third meaning, however, is substituted simply with 'law,' as visible among others from the above quotations. In *Grupo Mexicano* the phrase 'law and equity' is used as well. We follow this pattern in this section devoted to US law. See, e.g. Fletcher and Sheppard (2005), Chapter One.

not only in the legal system generally but specifically in the domain of provisional measures as well. This in particular because understanding the watershed decision of *Grupo Mexicano* case presumes this. Furthermore, this is needed also because for civil laws such dualism is foreign.

Actually, this is what brings us to the next historic miles stone, the adoption of the Federal Rules of Civil Procedure in 1938[9] and the impact that it had on American civil procedure, including our central subject matter—provisional measures. One of the leading US authorities epitomized the process as the period of '*struggle between law and equity and the subsequent coexistence of the systems*,'[10] the 1938 Rules being the line of demarcation. The integration, however, did not mean complete discarding of the division. What was achieved was rather only the merger of law and equity "*under a single set of simple and effective rules*."[11] Vestiges have survived up until today as illustrated, among others, by the area of law in the center of our observations to be shown below. In particular, the rule according to which, put simply, equitable provisional remedies (i.e., preliminary injunctions) could normally be awarded only if no adequate provisional remedy at common law is available, is the key rule of both, federal and State law on provisional measures.

In fact, one of the key reasons[12] why the majority of the US Supreme Court refused to recognize and introduce into US legal system the novel but related concept of the English Mareva Injunction in the watershed *Grupo Mexicano* case in 1999 was related exactly to the "*broad boundaries of traditional equitable relief*"[13] and the equitable powers of courts. The reasoning of the majority pointed to two quintessential related issues, both properly illustrating the continued relevance of the common law-equity dualism in American law. On the one hand, although preliminary injunctions as equitable provisional remedies are now enshrined in Rule 65 of Federal Rules of Civil Procedure, the majority was of the opinion that the courts' equitable powers do not grant them the power to introduce the Mareva Injunction-like local variant claimed by the petitioners—the "***all-purpose** prejudgment injunction.*" In other words, they were of the opinion that the scope and the contents of the US preliminary injunction,

[9]The Rules became effective on 16th of September 1938. For a succinct review of the road that led to the passage of the Rules see, e.g., Wright and Kane (2011), at 764.

[10]See Hazard (1985), title of section §1.5, at 14.

[11]Wright and Kane (2011), at 763.

[12]Besides the 'law & equity' line of argument, the other points supporting the decision of the majority of the Supreme Court included a number of other points. Two might properly illustrate them. On the one hand, it was brought up that the introduction of the local equivalent of Mareva would "*radically alter the balance between debtor's and creditor's rights which has been developed over centuries through many laws—icnluding those relating to bankruptcy, fraudulent conveyances, and preferences.*" On the other hand, the Court thought as well that the new device would generate a 'race to the courthouse' because "*any rational creditor would want to protect his investment [...] in cases involving insolvenyt or near-insolvent debtors, wjhich might prove financially fatal to the struggling debtor [...].*" Quoted from the *Grupo Mexicano* judgement.

[13]Id.

an equitable remedy otherwise recognized by American law, are much narrower than that of the English Mareva Injunction.[14]

On the other hand, the rejection to add such '*a new and powerful weapon to the creditor's arsenal*' was due also to the still applicable principle that "*an equitable remedy—a preliminary injunction—should not [be issued] when an adequate remedy at law exists.*"[15] The remedy at law that the US Supreme court deemed adequate is the **pre-judgment attachment**, which however provides inappropriate protection in numerous situations, as we will see below. These points properly show that American law on provisional measures continues to be significantly affected by the surviving dualism of common law and equity. Indeed, browsing through the relevent US scholarship, one could easily see that discussions on equity and equitable powers in the context of the law on provisional measures are among the central issues.[16]

The reason why the *Grupo Mexicano case* should be spoken of as an important point of orientation is because it became the alpha and omega not only for courts, both federal and States, but also to scholars, who felt urged—inspired by the words of Justice Scalia on the Mareva Injunction, the "*nuclear weapon of the law*"—to pick up the gauntlet and argue for or against the adaptation of the English success story provisional measure.

Finally, it needs to be added that the Rules—as amended quite frequently more recently[17]—have become a major success by now, however, not only on federal

[14]It ought to be noted that in the *Grupo Mexicano* case protection of the rights of *unsecured* creditors was only at stake and the Court did not rule on possible protection of rights of *secured* creditors and other lien-holders by the Mareva-like new powerful preliminary injunction claimed in the case. As secured creditors have rights in the collateral, preliminary injunctions are available to them and the restrictions of *Grupo Mexicano* do not apply to them. Preliminary injunctions therefore may be exploited to prevent the debtor to wrongfully hide or otherwise dispose of the assets used as collateral by secured creditors. See, e.g., the case *III Finance v. Aegis Consumer Funding Group, Inc.,* 1999 WL 461868 (S.D.N.Y. 1999), in which the court first issued a TRO *ex parte* and after a hearing also a preliminary injunction by reasoning that "*[t]he Grupo case is inapplicable here because III Finance claims a security interest in the assets subject to the preliminary injunction.*" Or, as the Supreme Court formulated in the case "*the substantive rule that a general creditor (one without a judgment) had no cognizable interest, either at law or in equity, in the property of his debtor, and therefore could not interfere with the debtor's use of that property.*" *Grupo Mexicano* at 319–320.

The holding of *Grupo Mexicano* therefore rests on the following four bases: (1) [district] courts lack the power to issue such preliminary injunctions, (2) that would prohibit defendant transferring specific assets, if (3) in such assets the claimant has no lien or equitable interest, (4) prior to entry of a money judgment.

[15]Wasserman (April 1992), at 306–7. (The author, on the one hand, criticizes the law by pointing to the limitations of American preliminary attachments and the encouraging experiences with the English Mareva Injunction and, on the other hand, it vouches for more frequent issuance of preliminary injunctions.

[16]See, e.g., Wasserman (1992) and the references in the article. The article of Wasserman was even cited by the Supreme Court in the *Grupo Mexicano* case. See also Burbank (2000), citing in note 1 Laycock (1993).

[17]A continuing body "*charged with the responsibility of examining the rules in action and recommending change[s]*" has existed since the reconstitution of the Advisory Committee (that drafted the Rules initially) in 1942. This body existed until 1956 when the Congress amended the Act to

level. As one of the leading comments highlighted "*[t]he excellence of the rules is such that in more than half the states the rules have been adapted for state use virtually unchanged, and there is not a jurisdiction that has not revised its procedure in some way that reflects the influence of the federal rules.*"[18] The key lesson thus is that federal and State laws on provisional measures are far from being complete strangers to each other though uniformity of civil procedure law throughout the country is yet to be achieved.[19] Hence, the ensuing discussion on federal law on provisional measures to a great extent is a discussion also on the laws of the States on this particular topic; and vice versa.

Now, let us briefly sketch the basic contours of the law in force.

3.2 Synopsys of US Law on Provisional Measures

3.2.1 The Federal Rules of Civil Procedure

As suggested already above, the primary remedy for securing satisfaction of a potential judgment is the preliminary (prejudgment) attachment. More precisely, as the underlying Rule 64 phrases it, remedies that provide for '*seizing a person*[20] *or property*' no matter how named and no matter whether State law requires an independent action.[21] The non-laundry list of Rule 64 mentions besides attachment also

create the Judicial Conference with the task of advising the Supreme Court on necessary changes. Wright and Kane (2011), at 765.

[18] *Id.* at 765.

[19] One of the factors that is looked upon as a 'threat to the integrity of the Civil Rules' and yet is of relevance to the law on preliminary measures is the proliferation of so-called 'local rules.' As initially it was presumed that "*these would be few in number and confined to purely housekeeping matters*," Rule 83 was added authorizing district courts to make such local rules. Contrary to expectations, however, they became extensive and covering "*a great variety of important matters.*" Moreover, they were a kind of trap to lawyers from other districts. Wright and Kane (2011), at 777. As a result, Rule 83 was amended in 1985 to ensure that local rules cannot step into force without being publicized and commented upon. *Id.* 778.

[20] The two provisional measure aimed at 'seizing a person,' abolished by most States, are the civil arrest and the writ of Ne Exeat. They served similar purposes. However, while the first was an order to the sheriff to arrest the defendant "*for the purpose of securing the defendant's court appearance on a certain day,*" the writ of Ne Exeat aimed "*to restrain the impending departure of a defendant from the jurisdiction of the court with the intent to evade its jurisdiction or to defraud the plaintiff.*" In both cases the defendant would be freed if he would post a bond. Where they still exists, they are rarely used, save the write of Ne Exeat in matrimonial cases. See Teply and Whitten (2013), at 669.

[21] See Rule 64(b).

arrest, garnishment,[22] replevin,[23] sequestration and "*other corresponding or equivalent remedies*." Although there are differences among these nominated remedies, their common denominator is that they "*focus on defendants who abscond, hide or convey assets, or leave the jurisdiction with intent to defraud creditors*"[24] and are characterized by having in rem effects.[25] This, in other words, means that they normally order the sheriff "*to seize tangible property, and to attach constructively the rest of the defendant's property*."[26] Only that particular type of these remedies may be resorted to at the commencement of and throughout an action that is available "*under the law of the [S]tate where the court is located*[27];" i.e., the forum state. Because of these features of American preliminary (prejudgment) attachments, they are essentially the functional equivalents of the French *saisie conservatoire* but not of the Mareva Injunction.

Although the preconditions for the issuance of preliminary attachment bear a resemblance to State laws and normally include demonstration of the probability of success on the merits, existence of extraordinary circumstances, the capability of proving of these is the litmus test for success or failure. As these factors are very fact and circumstance-specific, in-depth analysis of the related voluminous—otherwise instructive—case law clearly is beyond the confines of this paper. Last but not least, as a rule the preliminary (prejudgment) attachments may be issued ex parte only in "emergency situations"[28] or 'extraordinary circumstances'[29] unless otherwise pro-

---

[22]Garnishments differ from attachments in two key respects: first, the attached asset is seized from a third party (garnishee) and not from the hands of the debtor, and second, the garnishment can be both a prejudgment and a post-judgment remedy. See Tabb and Brubaker (2003a, b), at 41.

[23]Replevin (called, for example, in Louisiana sequestration) differs from attachment in that the "*creditor-plaintiff alleges a property right superior to the debtor in the very property seized [like a secured creditor seeking to enforce a security interest],*" which is not a requirement in case of either attachments or garnishments. Similarly, replevin can be a "s*tand alone action to recover property wrongfully distrained, [in contrast to attachment and garnishment], which are only ancillary to a main action for money damages.*" See Tabb and Brubaker (2003a, b), at 41.

[24]Teply and Whitten (2013), at 667.

[25]The seizure of persons per definition is an exception, however, as they have abandoned by the States, they may be left out of our discourse.

[26]Wasserman (1992), at 271.

[27]See Rule 64(a). Sequestration is, for example, a device known in Louisiana and the statutory preconditions for obtaining it are very similar to those on preliminary attachments in other States. It also may be issued e*x parte* (without notice to the debtor or opportunity for a hearing) when "*one claims the ownership or right to possession of property, or a mortgage, lien, or privilege thereon [and] if it is within the power of the defendant to conceal, dispose of, or waste the property or the revenues therefrom, or remove the property from the parish, during the pendency of the action.*" *Quoted* by the US Supreme Court in *Mitchell v. W.T. Grant Co.*, 410 U.S. 600. 94 S. Ct. 1895, 40 L. Ed. 2d 406 (1974).

[28]As Teply and Whitten put it, if "*the defendant is given a prompt post-seizure opportunity to challenge the order and writ, to substitute a bond (undertaking) for property attached or garnished, and to challenge the amount or sufficiency of the plaintiff's bond*." [Emphasis added.] Teply and Whitten (2013), at 667. According to some authors, they are as a rule issued e*x parte.* See, e.g., Tabb and Brubaker (2003a, b), at 42.

[29]See, e.g., *Colman v. Mertes* 408 N.W.2d 662 (Minn.App. 1987).

vided by the applicable State law. If one would like to ask the practical question of whether prejudgment attachments could easily be obtained, the reported cases suggest that the answer should rather be in the negative and preliminary (prejudgment) attachments are *not* issued routinely.[30]

Besides these in rem remedies, two types of preliminary equitable remedies with *in personam* effects are available to the movant parties: preliminary injunctions and temporary restraining orders (TROs). As such, similarly to the Mareva Injunction, they are "*personal orders to the defendant to do or refrain from doing some act*"[31] and may be requested either as the primary, or as a reserve option combined with a claim for a preliminary attachment.[32] No quantitative data seem to exist yet due to the primacy of preliminary attachments canvassed above, it seems that the latter tactical solution might be the wiser one to follow.[33] The tandem is regulated in some detail by Rule 65 of the Federal Rules of Civil Procedure, which applies generally and specifically also to copyright impoundments.[34] Contrary to Rule 64, Rule 54 does not require the federal court to apply the law and standards of the situs,[35] and this inevitably leads to differences in the approaches of not only federal but also State

[30] As an illustration see the case *Prospect Communications v. Herman* [2013 WL 6276816] adjudicated by US District Court D. Minnesota [not reported in F.Supp.2d (2013)] where the plaintiff's motion for a preliminary attachment was denied. In the case, the defendant instead of paying to the plaintiff for debts past due, was paying his debts to the tax authorities (IRS). To ensure satisfaction of any judgment to follow, plaintiff asked for a prejudgment attachment to seize the defendant's home and various accounts receivable. As some retailers (debtors of the defendant) stopped payments worth several million dollars to third persons and the plaintiff failed to prove that the defendant is attempting to hide assets, the court was of the opinion that the existence of extraordinary circumstances necessary for prejudgment attachment provisions were not proven.

[31] Teply and Whitten (2013), at 671.

[32] See, e.g., *Corporate Commission of the Mille Lacs Band of Ojibwe Indians v. Money Centers of American, Inc. and MCA of Wisconsin*, 915 F.Supp.2d 1059 (US District Court D. Minnesota). The plaintiff requested attachment of defendants assets or, alternatively, "*[enjoining] [the defendant] from dissipating assets allegedly belonging to the [Plantiff].*" While the attachment request was denied because out-of-jurisdiction assets were targeted and the "*Court [was] powerless to grant the requested relief,*" the preliminary injunction was denied because the claim was not equitable (rather "*fundamentally a contract dispute for money damages*").

[33] See, e.g., *Allstate Sales and Leasing Co., Inc. v. Geis,* 412 N.W.2d 30 (Minn. App., 1987). The case concerned a dispute that broke out between the former employer (Allstate)—a truck dealership—and some of its ex-employees when the former learned that the latter were in the process of acquiring a competing truck dealership. Allstate did not fire them immediately upon learning about that but only a bit later. However, it sued them for alleged wrongful unauthorized issuance of checks resulting of some alleged overpayments to some third parties. Allstate was awarded a TRO enjoining the spending of the overpayments and ordering depositing the amount with the court or in an escrow account. The TRO was quashed on the appellate level because Allstate "*failed to show it lacked an adequate legal remedy in the attachment statute or that it would be irreparably injured.*"

[34] See Rule 65(f).

[35] Shipley (2016), at 1171. Available at: http://digitalcommons.law.uga.edu/fac_artchop/1114. [Accessed 15 Apr. 2018].

courts notwithstanding that the same four criteria are employed on both levels when ruling on motions for preliminary injunctions.[36]

The key differences between preliminary injunctions and TROs are the following. *First,* only the latter may be issued ex parte subject to satisfaction of some statutory requirements.[37] *Secondly*, although both are issued for a limited period of time, while the TROs expire within 14 days,[38] the preliminary injunctions are issued until the final resolution of the case on the merits. *Thirdly,* the TROs assist the preliminary injunctions because they function to "*preserve the status quo until there can be a hearing on a preliminary injunction.*"[39] *Fourthly,* different standards of irreparable harm apply for the two. As one court put it, while a court granting a preliminary injunction needs to find that "*the failure to grant it would result in irreparable harm,*" [emphasis added] it is sufficient that irreparable harm *might* result from not awarding a TRO.[40] It is a common requirement, however, that for their issuance the moving party must provide a security of value sufficient to pay the potential costs and damages sustained by the affected parties.[41]

This tandem, even if only conditionally, may be taken to be the American concept most closely related to the English Mareva Injunction (freezing orders), rather than the latter only. Hence, as a meaningful part of scholars having compared the two systems have restricted themselves to the comparison of the Mareva Injunction to American preliminary injunctions—without the ancillary TROs—their findings may not tell the full story.

What is not visible from the text of the federal Rules of Civil Procedure is whether the preliminary (prejudgment) attachments and preliminary injunctions could be resorted to cumulatively or in any particular order? As far as the first part of the question is concerned, the case law and scholars equally support the view that US courts (both federal and State) generally refuse to cumulate them.[42] This is primarily

[36]*Id.* The four factors are: "*(1) the threat that the moving party will suffer irreparable injury if the injunction is not granted; (2) the moving party's likelihood of success on the merits; (3) the possible hardships to the moving party if the injunction is not granted outweigh the possible harm to the defendant if the injunction is granted (also called the balance of equities); and (4) granting of injunction will be in the public interest.*" *Id.* note 4, at 1171.

[37]See Rule 65(b)(1), according to which the court may issue the TRO 'without written or oral notice to the adverse party or its attorney' if "*specific facts in an affidavit or a verified complaint clearly show that immediate and irreparable injury, loss, or damage will result to the movant before the adverse party can be heard in opposition,*" and "*the movant's attorney certifies in writing any efforts made to give notice and the reasons why it should not be given.*".

[38]Rule 65(b)(2). The expiry date set by the court may be extended by the judge for good cause for a similar period of time. Likewise, the adverse party may agree for a longer extension. *Id.*

[39]Teply and Whitten (2013), at 671. See also Rule 65(b)(3).

[40]See *Byrd v. Ritchie Grocer Co.,* decided by Court of Appeals of Arkansas (1985 WL 12622; not reported in S.W.2d [1985]).

[41]Rule 65(c).

[42]Wasserman (1992), at 306–7. See, also, *for example, In Re Philip R. Cohn v. David E. Lyon,* 11 B.R. 611 (1981). In the case, bankruptcy trustee asked the court to issue both, a preliminary attachment and a preliminary injunction. The case involved recovery of money allegedly loaned by bankrupt to his brother-in-law. While the attachment of brother-in-law's real estate was granted by

to be attributed to the already mentioned equitable principle, corroborated by the Supreme Court's judgment in *Grupo Mexicano,* according to which whenever adequate remedy at law is available, equitable ones should not awarded. Consequently, normally only preliminary (prejudgment) attachments are awarded and preliminary injunctions are reserved only for rare extraordinary cases.[43] Moreover, some courts, presumably influenced by the logic and spirit of *Grupo Mexicano,* "*have hesitated or refused to grant preliminary injunctions to freeze a defendant's assets in actions in which the plaintiff sought only money damages, even though she may have met the traditional requirements for preliminary injunctive relief*."[44]

Last but not least, to the list of reasons why courts hesitated or refused granting of preliminary injunctions one should also add the constraint of precedents.[45] It is sufficient here to recall the impact the *Grupo Mexicano* case had in which Justice Scalia and the majority reasoned not only that an "*all-purpose prejudgment injunction [...] could render Federal Rule of Civil Procedure 64, which authorizes use of state prejudgment remedies, a virtual irrelevance*," but also that it is the Congress that is in the best position to "*design an appropriate remedy*"[46] and not the courts. The end result is thus that, contrary to the Mareva Injunction, preliminary injunctions are reserved to very exceptional cases only and are subjected to quite demanding court-made standards on which additionally there is no full agreement between federal and State courts.[47]

3.2.2 State Law Variations

Much of what has been said above on federal law, applies also on the State level given that most of the States have taken over the Rules, or at least have been inspired by them. Discrepancies do exist, however, among the various States. Three of them

the court, the preliminary injunction was not because "*preliminary injunction could not be granted without further hearing or stipulation.*" A similar pattern was applied in the already cited case of the *Federal Trade Commission* et al. *as plaintiffs and Fortune Hi-Tech Marketing Inc.* et al. Civil No. 13 CV 578 (issued on 24th of January 2013 at 1:45 p.m. by US District Court for the Northern District of Illinois, Eastern Division).

[43]DiSarro (2011), at 53.

[44]Wasserman (1992), at 306.

[45]Wasserman (1992), at 306.

[46]See *Grupo Mexicano,* majority opinion stating as well that "*the equitable powers conferred by the Judiciary Act of 1789 [on courts] did not include the power to create remedies previously unknown to equity jurisprudence. [Therefore,] [e]ven if sitting as a court of equity, [the US Supreme court has] no authority to craft a 'nuclear weapon' of the law like the one advocated [by the petitioners in the case].*"

[47]Courts, generally, consider the following four factors when deciding on preliminary injunctions: (1) the likelihood of the claimant's success on the merits; (2) the injury claimant may sustain if preliminary injunction is denied; (3) balance between the possible injury of the applicant versus the "*possible injury to the opposing party,*" and (4) whether "*the public interest would be harmed by issuance of a preliminary injunction.*" Teply and Whitten (2013), at 672.

will be briefly mentioned here. *Firstly*, there are significant differences between the designations and the typology of provisional measures of the various States.[48] These should be borne in mind when researching this area of law to avoid misunderstandings. *Secondly*, the direction given in *Grupo Mexicano* has not been uniformly followed by the various States' courts.[49] While some courts remained within the limits of the ruling, others were willing to interpret it more loosely. New York seems to have been the proponent of the first position.[50] *Thirdly*, some State courts extended the traditional boundaries of provisional measures law; as Illinois did at least in one case involving prejudgment attachments.[51]

It ought to be mentioned here as well that discrepancies exist also between the position of State and federal courts. As the Mareva Injunction is being taken as our primary benchmark, it is important to mention the divergence of standards State (and federal) courts employ when deciding on awarding of preliminary injunctions. Namely, although "*most federal and [S]tate courts weigh roughly the same four criteria in ruling on motions for provisional relief [...] courts in some jurisdictions evaluate the factors on a sliding scale or with a balancing test while some federal circuits require the moving party to establish each of them.*"[52]

3.2.3 Constitutional Due Process Limitations Common to Prejudgment Remedies

The overview of US law on provisional remedies would not be complete without a gloss on a series of US Supreme Court cases starting with the 1969 *Sniadach v. Family Finance Corp. case*[53] that narrowed down the possibilities for issuance of ex parte measures considerably. These were all related to due process considerations

---

[48] For example, the new Civil Procedure Code of Louisiana of 2017 (Arts. 3501–3613) lists attachment, garnishment, sequestration as well as in personam TROs and preliminary injunctions. In Florida, for example, prejudgment writ of replevin is known (Chapter 78, Section 78.068) or injunction against removal of mortgaged personal property (Chapter 60, Section 60.03, Title VI Civil Practice and Procedure of Florida Statutes). For a list of links to State civil procedure acts or codes see https://www.law.cornell.edu/wex/table_civil_procedure.

[49] The Uniform Law Commission's (2012) Summary of the Uniform Asset Preservation Orders Act highlighted this problem as follows: "*Some [S]tate supreme courts concluded, in the wake of] the Grupo Mexicano decision], that courts in their [S]tate lacked the authority to issue those types of of orders* [i.e., *preliminary injunctions*]. *At least one supreme court concluded the opposite.*"

[50] A New York court rejected awarding of a Mareva-style relief to claimants of money damages in the case *Credit Agricole Indosuez v. Rossiyskiy Kredit Bank,* 729 N.E.2d 683, 689 (N.Y. 2000).

[51] As opposed to that an Illinois federal court held that the preliminary attachment available under Illinois' law "*can be extended to assets outside the jurisdiction granting the authority.*" See *MX Distrib Co v. Web Records Inc.*, 2003 US Dist. LEXIS 9092 (N.D. III. 2003). Both cited by Hoyle (2006), note 112, at 212.

[52] Shipley (2016), at 1171. Consequently, the standards of the State and federal court with the same situs may not be the same; as opposed to the standards applicable for prejudgment attachments.

[53] 395 U.S. 337, 89 S.Ct. 1820, 23 L. Ed. 2d 349 (1969).

enshrined in the 14th Amendment of the US Constitution. Although the road leading to the ultimately still valid rules was a bit winding,[54] the focal point for us here is that while prejudgment remedies have not become unconstitutional per se, the normal requirement is notice and opportunity for an adversary proceeding. The ordering of preliminary measures ex parte, however, has become radically narrowed down and subject to an intricate 'due process matrix.'[55] This development in US law seems to be in stark contrast with the expansion of the Mareva Injunction, for example.

3.2.4 *The Uniform Asset-Protection Orders Act 2012*

A brief mention of the Uniform Asset-Protection Orders Act of 2012,[56] a soft law instrument drafted by the Uniform Law Commission, is essential in this context because its bypassing would make the overall picture on American law on preliminary measures incomplete. Namely, as the drafters themselves admitted, the project leading to the act was triggered by the fact that the "*viability of asset-preservation orders was called into question by the decision of the United States Supreme Court in Grupo Mexicano [...].*"[57] Consequently, "*[a]lthough, the Grupo Mexicano decision involved the jurisdiction of the federal courts, it caused some confusion in the state court system over the propriety of asset-preservation orders.*"[58] While most

---

[54]Two cases on the topic were adjudicated by the Supreme Court in an unusually narrow timeframe of two years. Namely, while *Fuentes v. Shevin* (407 U.S. 67, 92 S. Ct. 1983, 32 L. Ed. 2d 556) was decided in 1972, *Mitchell v. Grant* (416 U.S. 600, 94 S. Ct. 1895, 40 L. Ed. 2d 406) is from 1974. Although two different States (in Fuentes Florida, in Mitchell Louisiana) and the constitutionality of two different remedies were at stake (in Fuentes, pre-judgment garnishment, in Mitchell sequestration and vendor's lien), the issues presented closely resembled. The above matrix essentially grew out of these two cases, as refined though later. As the dissenters in Mitchell suggested, the Supreme Court granted certiorari in Mitchell so that it could rectify the errors made in Fuentes and that is the reason for the narrow time frame between the two cases.

[55]The requirements include (1) "a *factual affidavit or other sworn statement by someone with personal knowledge showing that the grounds for issuing the remedy exists*;" (2) a judge rather than a clerk of a court may only issue ex parte measures; and (3) the defendant must be given the opportunity to be heard and to contest the issued measure as soon as possible (prompt post-seizure hearing). See Teply and Whitten (2013), at 677. Not a requirement, but the constitutionality of an *ex parte* provisional remedy "*will be more secure if* (1) *it is sought for the seizure of property in which the plaintiff has a pre-existing interest, and* (2) *the plaintiff's claim is subject to documentary proof, rather than being dependent upon the testimony of witnesses about (perhaps complex) past events.*" *Id.* at 677–78. The pre-existing interest is, for example, a security interest (e.g., pledge, mortgage).

[56]The text of the uniform act is available electronically at http://www.uniformlaws.org/shared/docs/asset_freezing_orders/UAPOA_Final%20Act_2014.pdf. [Accessed on 26 Aug. 2017.].

[57]UCL, Asset Preservation Orders Act Summary, available electronically at http://www.uniformlaws.org/ActSummary.aspx?title=Asset-Preservation%20Orders%20Act. [Accessed on 28 Aug. 2017]. [Hereinafter: UAPOA Summary.].

[58]*Id.* UAPOA Summary.

State Supreme Courts followed the holding of *Grupo Mexicano*, at least one was of contrary opinion.

Although the central aim of the uniform act is to provide a panacea against such confusion caused by the *Grupo Mexicano ruling* through a hoped-for harmonization of State laws, implicitly the act is also an affirmative answer to the initial question leading to the *Grupo Mexicano* holding of whether a Mareva Injunction-type of preliminary remedy is needed in US law. The prefatory notes and comments on the uniform act justify that by three main reasons: first, the experiences of such "*well-developed sources*" as English or Canadian laws,[59] secondly, the fact that American courts have themselves issued such injunctions before *Grupo Mexicano*, and thirdly, by pointing to the deficiencies of preliminary attachments as '*the primary remedy against asset dissipation*'[60] as per law in force. The notes, however, mention as the determinative deficiency of preliminary attachments the fact that they "*[...] [apply] only to assets which are within the jurisdiction of the court and which are known to the party seeking prejudgment attachment. [...]*"[61] and do not go beyond that.

It is to be noted additionally that hidden in the notes and comments a fourth, public international law-type of reason was put forward by the drafters as well. As they put it "*Grupo Mexicano also placed the United States at odds with other common law countries, which permit so-called Mareva or similar type injunctions, because reciprocity of enforcement has become a priority when assets may be transferred instantly with the push of a button.*" Namely, the act not only proclaims but also sets the preconditions for recognition[62] not only of asset preservation orders made by the various States but also by "*courts outside the United States.*"[63] This seems to be a highly desirable international path-setting formula for recognition of foreign freezing orders to be followed by others as well.

Contents-wise, the uniform act has relied on the experiences with temporary restraining orders and preliminary injunctions.[64] For that reason those knowledgeable in this area of law will hardly find surprising novelties in the act's provisions. The key features of the orders are that they have *in personam* effects,[65] are applicable

---

[59] *Id.* UAPOA Summary.

[60] UAPOA prefatory notes and comments, at 2. Note that the prefatory notes precede the text of UAPOA in the version available electronically at the website of the Uniform Law Commission.

[61] UAPOA prefatory notes and comments, at 2. Preliminary attachments suffer from other deficiencies as well though subject to variation from State to State. For example, in Pennsylvania this remedy is not available neither in federal or state court in this state as the related statutory provisions were rescinded, in many other States it is available only in certain particular kinds of cases or some limits are placed on what kinds of property may be attached. See Wasserman 1992, at 277.

[62] UAPOA Arts. 8(c) and 8(d). The first, for example, foresees that the order may not be recognized by a US court if it was issued by a foreign court not having personal or *in rem* jurisdictions or if it "*was rendered under a judicial system that does not provide impartial tribunals or procedures compatible with the requirements of due process of law.*"

[63] UAPOA Art. 8(b).

[64] *Id. See also* UAPOA Summary.

[65] As the prefatory note to the UAPOA states: "*An asset-preservation order is injunctive relief, applying* in personam, *which preserves assets by preventing their dissipation so that sufficient*

only in case of actions for monetary damages,[66] may be issued ex parte[67] and subject to the already known "*rigorous process for issuance*[68];"—including the court's right to ask posting of a bond.[69]

While the fact that the initiative for launching the project leading to the Uniform Act was subscribed to by the Uniform Law Commission undoubtedly proves that many think there is a need not only for a uniform law on preliminary freezing orders but also for a Mareva-type remedy, the failure to enact the statutory (hard law) version of the act by any of the States by now points in the opposite direction. It remains to be seen whether meaningful changes will occur on this front in the near future perhaps as a result of the increasing international regulatory competition in the domain; at the moment led by the 'nuclear weapon of the law'—the English Mareva Injunction.

3.3 Mareva Injunctions and the US System of Provisional Measures: Differences and Commonalities

3.3.1 The American Provisional Measures v. the English Mareva Injunction: The Main Inherent Limitations of the American System

US literature is understandably primarily focused on the comparative disadvantages of preliminary attachments as those provisional measures that are as a rule awarded by US courts; as was explained above. Therefore, they are primarily contrasted to the Mareva Injunction and the following main comparative disadvantages of the American prejudgment attachments are typically highlighted. For some reason, the fact that preliminary attachments create liens—*inchoate liens*—is given less attention and it is harder to determine whether this particular feature of attachments is to be perceived as an advantage or disadvantage. A brief comment nonetheless is required on that point, too.

First, US courts cannot attach foreign assets, including not only assets located in another State but also assets in a non-US jurisdiction.[70] Consequently, for proper protection the moving party would have to launch court proceedings in such other State(s) as the forum where valuable assets of the debtor are located, which would obviously

---

assets will be available to satisfy an existing or future judgment. Because an asset-preservation order is in the nature of injunctive relief, violations of the order are punishable by contempt." [Emphasis added.].

[66] UAPOA Art. 4(a).

[67] UAPOA Art. 5. The act speaks of ex parte measures as 'orders issued without notice.'

[68] *Id.* UAPOA Arts. 4, 5 and 7.

[69] UAPOA Art. 7.

[70] Wasserman (1992), at 277.

entail increased costs, inconvenience and enhanced liability exposure (risks).[71] *Secondly*, some States limit attachment to specific explicitly listed claims (e.g., contractual claims).[72] Here, it suffices only to note that as opposed to such 'limitations of the geographic reach of the attachment' and 'subject matter restrictions of the attachment,'[73] today we live in the era when the enforceability of *worldwide* Mareva Injunctions is what is being tested.

Thirdly, Wasserman mentions a third group of limitations as well under the heading of '*intrusiveness of attachment*.'[74] This characteristic of prejudgment attachments, however, may be looked upon not only as a deficiency but also as a strength (advantage) that perfectly fits the goal of ensuring enforceability of the future judgment. Wasserman lists under this heading some manifestations of the changed strategic position of the parties generated by preliminary attachments. Presumably the two most important manifestations of the attachments' intrusion are all the downsides of dispossessing the debtor of certain property through the fact that attachment may trigger a technical mortgage default and affect the debtor's credit rating.[75] Yet as both preliminary attachments and preliminary injunctions serve eventually the same end of ensuring that the plaintiff prevailing in a trial could collect on the judgment, preliminary injunctions obviously are just as intrusive though in different forms and with different intensity. As dispossessing the debtor is the gist of the French *Saisie* and one of the Hungarian provisional measures, these thoughts apply *mutatis mutandis* also to them.

Lastly, a brief digression on *inchoate liens* created by prejudgment attachments. These are *inchoate*, not fully-fledged liens because their generators, preliminary attachments are also only temporary. Their temporary nature notwithstanding, they represent priorities that are valid both within and outside bankruptcy proceedings and thus a creditor having such an inchoate lien may trump a lower ranking lien of a different sort. In other words, theoretically they may be valuable should bankruptcy proceedings be launched against the defendant or in case of conflict of liens on the same asset of the debtor. The utility of inchoate liens seems to have escaped even the attention US scholars, let alone the systems that do not even k recognise such effects. At any event, to the extent if in such priority conflicts inchoate liens are of use, this particular feature of US preliminary attachments should be perceived as an advantage that is not a corollary of Mareva Injunctions. Yet this advantage admittedly is an asset only in the US where the bankruptcy systems works and where the number of bankruptcy proceedings launched annually has been the highest in the world yet it may mean little elsewhere where this is not so.

Interestingly, the attachment lien created by preliminary attachments is looked upon by some authors as a disadvantage, though based on dubious presumptions. This line of argument presumes a certain type of behaviour by the other creditors of

[71] Tabb and Brubaker (2003a, b), at 47.

[72] See, e.g., Cal. Civ. Proc. Code §§ 483.010, 492.010 (2006).

[73] These designations were borrowed from Wasserman. See Wasserman (1992), at 276–77.

[74] Wasserman (1992), at 281.

[75] Wasserman (1992), at 281–82.

the debtor whose assets were seized and on which an inchoate lien was established. Such presumptions may but must not materialize in real life. The central contention is that the other competing creditors, once faced with the issued preliminary attachment, are incentivized to promptly "*protect themselves by forcing the debtor into involuntary bankruptcy*,"[76] hoping that it may be avoided by the trustee. Yet neither is avoidance something automatic in US bankruptcy law, nor are other creditors necessarily interested in attacking the lien otherwise created fully according to the law.

Last but not least, as preliminary injunctions are issued only very exceptionally and therefore the related case law inevitably is limited, it makes scant sense to compare them to the Mareva Injunctions. This will change once the system would elevate them from their inferior position and make out of them functionally different but equal provisional remedies with preliminary attachments.

3.3.2 The American Provisional Measures v. the English Mareva Injunction: Policy and Practical Differences

For a proper comparison of two laws the mechanical juxtaposition of their applicable statutory frameworks is hardly sufficient. It is also inevitably essential to identify those main comparative advantages of the English Mareva Injunction that make it more powerful than the entire tri-partite system of US provision measures. It seems that three such practical and policy-based differences should in particular be mentioned in this specific context. Let's start first with two policy points, to conclude with the most practical dilemma corollary to the existence of any kind of provisional measures: assessment of whether the provisional measures are realistically within the reach of the parties?

Firstly, the policies of the two jurisdictions radically differ as far as their approach to ex parte provisional measures is concerned. Here, it suffices only to summarize what has already been said above starting with the fact that ex parte provisional measures are known in both countries. However, while in the US ex parte provisional measures are exceptional—moreover caught by the restraints formulated by the US Supreme Court in the mentioned post-Sniadach series of cases[77]—the English Mareva Injunctions are normally issued, indeed, ex parte.[78] The pro-ex parte English stance is well-expressed by Hoyle suggesting that in the UK it is commonly subscribed to that "[…] *without notice application is … vital, as it is hardly consistent with the fear of a defendant dissipating his assets if not restrained, to give him*

---

[76]Wasserman (1992), at 284.

[77]See the ensuing sub-section discussing this topic.

[78]This notwithstanding that as per Rule 25.3(1) of the CPR they court may but must not grant an interim remedy "*on an application made without notice if it appears to the court that there are good reasons for not giving notice.*"

advance notice of the hearing."[79] The best evidence that such an approach has not caused major problems, as he added, is that the number of applications to discharge freezing orders is '*comparatively rare.*'[80]

As opposed to the milder policy differences on ex parte measures, *secondly*, the two Anglo-Saxon systems' policies more radically point in opposite directions as far as their approaches to the development of the law of provisional measures is concerned. As already suggested, the US Supreme Court has reiterated its 'static approach' to preliminary injunctions in a series of post-*Grupo Mexicano* decisions, making these pre-judgment remedies extraordinary, "*a drastic provisional remedy that should be sparingly granted.*"[81] Put simply, neither making preliminary injunctions generally available, nor expanding their contents is possible. Furthermore, the same static approach seems to dominate also the law of preliminary attachments though perhaps in this domain some courts seem to have been more willing to break the confines; presumably in the lack of restraining language of the *Grupo Mexicano* type. As opposed to such 'static approach' of American law, the relatively brief history of the Mareva Injunction was nothing else but constant expansion. As opposed to the initial position, Mareva or its legal success the Freezing Order, are today neither an exceptional remedy, nor limited to use in 'shipping and commercial circles'[82] only, or constrained to the UK.

Last but not least, perhaps the most determinative issue for any comparative analysis of preliminary measures relates to the ease with which such remedies could be obtained in courts of law. In the lack of a commonly accepted formula for expressing this determinant with exact quantitative data, or other tools of empirical research, one cannot but rely on the opinions of renowned experts. Here, thus we will content ourselves by referring to the US scholars Brubaker and Tabb whose qualifications might be sufficiently expressive of this peculiar distinguishing factor. As they submit, while the American "*[p]rejudgment remedies are disfavoured, and are hard to get [and] [t]hey are the exception, and not the rule,*[83] *[...] [i]n England, [preliminary injunctions], known there as 'Mareva injunctions, are becoming increasingly routine.*"[84] This notwithstanding that "*[t]he granting or denial of injunctive relief is addressed to the sound discretion of the Court*"[85] in the US as well. Given that US courts normally award only preliminary attachments and preliminary injunctions in very rare cases only, as explained above, this opinion of Brubaker and Tabb means that while it is *hard* to get a preliminary attachment, it is even *considerably harder* to obtain a preliminary injunction.

---

[79]Hoyle (2006), para 1.22, at 8.

[80]*Id.*

[81]DiSarro (2011), at 53.

[82]Hoyle (2006), para 1.12, at 4.

[83]Tabb and Brubaker (2003a, b), at 40.

[84]Tabb and Brubaker (2003a, b), at 47.

[85]See, e.g., *State Bank & Trust Company v. Hambone's Corporation*, (Court of Common Please, Summit County, Ohio, case No: 2001-11-5455) citing *Perkins v. Quaker City* (1956) 165 Ohio St. 120 (Syllabus).

These differences and the restraints featuring US law notwithstanding, it would be erroneous to go too far in our conclusions. Namely, as one source concluded, "*while American courts have not embraced the 'nuclear weapon of the Mareva injunction* per se, *they are not without other devastating devices in practice*."[86]

3.3.3 The Tokens of Efficiency of the American System

Similarly to the UK, contempt of court rules—and perhaps even more their quite rigorous enforcement—are the key factors behind the efficiency of the American provisional measures. More precisely, as attachment presumes seizure of a defendant's property, contempt of court—civil or criminal—plays a role rather only in case of TROs and preliminary injunctions. Both civil and criminal contempt may be resorted to by the court as the basic rule is that "*[t]he nature and purpose of the sanction imposed […] determines the kind of contempt involved in the case*."[87] This is similar to the role contempt of court plays in enforcing Mareva Injunctions in England. If observed only locally (from within the system), the pivotal role contempt of court rules play generally and specifically ensuring TROs and preliminary injunctions work may not be visible. However, when one takes a look at some of the less developed legal systems even of Continental Europe, it becomes visible how quintessential this particular building block of the legal system plays, among others, in making provisional measures something to be taken seriously.

Besides the contempt of court rules, two further less noted facets of US law should be mentioned, though leaving the exploration of these topics to future scholarship. On the one hand, the American provisional measures work efficiently also because they may be combined with a number of other legal remedies,[88] the *synergic effect* of

---

[86] Jeffrey (2005), at 726. Available at: http://scholarship.law.stjohns.edu/jcred/vol19/iss3/. [Accessed on 15 Apr. 2018]. Wilson drew the above conclusion based on the following cases: *In Re Estate of Ferdinand Marcos, Human Rights Litig.*, 25 F.3d 1467, 1478 (9th Cir. 1994) [affirming temporary injunction to enjoin Estate from transferring, secreting, or dissipating Estate's assets pending litigation]; *MS Distrib Co v. Web Records Inc.*, 2003 US Dist. LEXIS 9092; *Philips Med. Sys. Int'l B.V.*, 8 F.3d (7th Cir. 1993) [affirming order to the defendant to deposit money into court prior to final judgment]; *Rep. of the Philippines v. Marcos*, 862 F2d.1355, 1364 (9th Cir. 1988) [affirming freezing order prohibiting defendants from dissipating assets not within the US territorial jurisdiction] and *Fed. Trade Comm'n v. Verity Int'l*, 2001 US Dist. LEXIS 6097 (S.D.N.Y. 2001) [denying defendant's motion to vacate or modify preliminary injunction]. *Cited also by* Hoyle (2006), note 113, at 212.

[87] Teply and Whitten (2013), at 674.Criminal contempt sanctions—either fixed fines or fixed jail sentences—"*are imposed to punish someone for violating a court decree in order to vindicate the court's authority*." Civil contempt sanctions, on the other hand, aim to "*coerce compliance with the court's order in the future*." Another difference between the two relates to the right to a trial by jury: while imposing of serious penalties for criminal contempt requires trial by jury, that is not a requirement in case of civil contempt sanctions. *Id.*

[88] See, e.g., the already mentioned case of *FTC v. Fortune Hi-Tech Marketing Inc.* et al. Civil No. 13 CV 578 (issued on 24th of January 2013 at 1:45 p.m. by US District Court for the Northern District of Illinois, Eastern Division), which (1) ex parte TRO with asset freeze, (2) appointment of a receiver,

which could not only match but even surpass the effects of the Mareva Injunction if not accompanied by supporting tools (e.g., ancillary search orders allowing inspection of documents and premises of the debtor).[89] This is to a great degree possible because of the permissive procedural rules on joinder of claims[90] and cumulating of remedies; something which is either not possible or is significantly limited in many other jurisdictions.

On the other hand, the freedom with which courts may shape the contents of provisional measures may not exist in many other jurisdictions either. Yet such 'equitable discretion'[91] is of crucial importance to allow courts to impose those kinds of orders that would best fit the needs of the circumstances of the case at hand; even more if necessary. This may not be so in less developed legal systems, where a kind of straight jacket is imposed on judges actually forcing them to impose only a few settled types of orders no matter how ill-suited they may be in some cases.

Admittedly, these comparative advantages of US law may not necessarily be conspicuous from within the system. However, if observed from the perspective of such other foreign jurisdictions the civil procedure laws of which tolerate, neither such cumulating of various remedies, nor provide freedom to judges to tailor the preliminary injunctions to the needs of the concrete cases, one should realize that these thoughts deserve merit.

---

and (3) some other equitable relief was asked. For example, the court imposed certain duties on such third parties as well, which held defendants' assets, as well as prohibition of disclosure customer information, and duty to maintain records and report new business activity. These all were necessary given that the case was about a major pyramid scheme.

[89]It is not without reason that scholars and commentators of the law on Mareva Injunctions (freezing orders) underline that "*[a] skilful choice of ancillary orders makes both Search and Freezing Orders even more powerful weapons in a claimant's armoury*." See Hoyle (2006), para 8.1, at 115.

[90]Federal Rules of Civil Procedure Rule 18 on Joinder of Claims stating as a general rule that "*A party asserting a claim, counterclaim, crossclaim, or third-party claim may join, as independent or alternative claims, as many claims as it has against an opposing party*." Though as per Rule 42 the court may order separate trials for one or more claims 'for convenience, to avoid prejudice, or to expedite and economize.' See also Rule 54(b) according to which the court must adjudicate all claims (but may decide on some earlier) and Rule 54(c)—allowing for cumulating of remedies—spelling out that "*Every ... final judgment should grant the relief to which each party is entitled, even if the party has not demanded that relief in its pleadings*."

[91]As Wasserman phrased, "*[...] rather than barring the defendant from making any transfers whatsoever, the court can preliminary enjoin the defendant only from making transfers outside the ordinary course of business, Or the court can freeze all assets except those needed for ordinary living expenses or attorney's fees. Or it can modify or vacate the injunction if the defendant posts a bond to ensure satisfaction of the plaintiff's expected money judgement. Exercising this equitable discretion, courts can accommodate the defendant's basic needs without risking irreparable tertiary harm to the plaintiff. [...]*." *Quoted from* Wasserman (1992), at 297–98.

3.4 Positioning US Law

As the above discussion hopefully showed, one cannot deny that US law possesses more provisional remedies that together with the contempt of court rules and other available civil procedure tools work efficiently in practice; something that is only wishful thinking in many other jurisdictions. Still, compared to the English Mareva Injunction, it is a legitimate question that desires further exploration whether seizure of defendant's assets is an appropriate substitute for an injunction "limited to" prohibiting certain actions by the debtor especially if coupled with ancillary search orders?[92]

The persuasive force of the *concurring* and *dissenting* opinions in *Grupo Mexicano* itself (notwithstanding their limitations),[93] the lively scholarly discourse that emanated from the case, and ultimately the fact that in 2012 the Uniform Asset-Protection Orders Act drafted by the Uniform Law Commission has seen the daylight, suggest that the US law on provisional measures is far from being perfect either. Most importantly, as a Japanese professor noted, English pragmatism surrounding the growth of jurisprudence on Mareva Injunction was not paralleled in the US because of Justice Scalia's "*restrictive approach [was driven by] his motive to curb the judicial activism since the latter half of the 20th century.*"[94] As a global path-setter in law it is problematic as well that "*[a]lthough it is theoretically possible to obtain a provisional relief from a U.S. court to aid the main proceedings in a foreign country, such course of action is fraught with uncertainty and delay.*"[95]

It should not be a too futuristic thought therefore to consider that preliminary injunctions are not only the second best option but an equal alternative to preliminary attachments, too. This notwithstanding that the *Grupo Mexicano* ruling withheld all the challenges so far and irrespective that at the moment nothing seems to suggest that the Uniform Asset-Protection Orders Act will metamorphose from soft to hard law in the near future. The timing of the debate in the Congress on the equivalent of Mareva—'*this formidable power over debtors*'[96]—as suggested by Justice Scalia

---

[92] Sandrock argued in 1987 that the English Mareva and US prejudgment attachments functionally are very similar as they "*[satisfy] the same procedural needs.*" Sandrock (Winter 1987), at 11. [He recommends international lenders to acquire express waivers of immunity from their sovereign borrowers to ensure that they can resort to provisional measures.] Id. at 42.

[93] David Capper criticized not only the majority but also the concurring and dissenting minority in *Grupo Mexicano* not only for the "*awful job of explaining why the Mareva injunction should not be part of the remedial machinery of the federal courts,*" but also for having improperly briefed the pertaining English law as visible from the opinion of the minority. As he put it: "*Not even the opinion of the minority reveals a clear understanding of what a Mareva injunction is.*" One cannot but side also with his note that in fact there was no reason for granting certiorari either. Capper (2005), at 2180.

[94] Tamaruya (2010), at 367.

[95] Park (2017), at 1001 (The author argues for a treaty-based solution of the problem.).

[96] As the majority in *Grupo Mexicano* formulated, "*[t]he debate concerning this formidable power over debtors should be conducted and resolved where such issues belong in our democracy: in the Congress,*" rather than by courts.

and the majority in *Grupo Mexicano*—likewise is unknown at this point in time. The voices of the industry pointing in the opposite direction[97] have so far failed to change this.

References

Domestic Law: United States

California Civil Procedure Code (2006)
Civil Procedure Code of Louisiana of 2017
Federal Rules of Civil Procedure (1938)
Florida Civil Practice and Procedure

US Soft Law

Uniform Law Commission (2012) Uniform Asset-Preservation Orders Act

Books

Fletcher PG, Sheppard S (2005) American law in a global context: the basics. Oxford University Press
Gilmore G (1977) The ages of American law. Yale University Press
Hazard J (1985) Civil procedure, 3rd edn. Little, Brown & Co., Boston-Toronto
Hoyle MSW (2006) Freezing and search orders, 4th edn. Informa-London
Tabb JCh, Brubaker R (2003a) Bankruptcy law—principles, policies, and practice. Anderson Publ, Cincinnati
Tabb JCh, Brubaker R (2003b) Bankruptcy law—principles, policies, and practice. Anderson Publ, Cincinnati
Teply LL, Whitten RU (2013) Civil procedure, 5th edn. Carolina Academic Press
Wright SC, Kane MK (2011) Law of federal courts. West Academic Publishing (Hornbook Series) (2017)

[97]See, e.g., Kirschner and Silverman (2002). [Accessed on 15 Apr. 2018]. The authors were of the opinion that "*Mareva orders do have a place in the United States*," among others, because such orders would be of tremendous use also in the context of bankruptcy proceedings. Namely, while application of avoidance laws of bankruptcy law (involving often also litigation) "*takes a tremendous amount of time and absorbs a tremendous amount of money that would otherwise be available to creditors*," Mareva orders would be the means to prevent avoidable transactions before bankruptcy.

Articles

Barrack LD, Bolton DJ, Flom LB (2011) Grupo Mexicano: Has Picard Resurrected the Right to Pre-Judgment Attachments? Am Bankruptcy Inst J 52–53

Burbank BS (2000) The bitter with the sweet: tradition, history, and limitations on federal judicial power—a case study. Notre Dame Law Rev 75(4):1291–1346

Capper D (2005) The need for Mareva injunctions reconsidered. 73 Fordham Law Rev 2161

DiSarro A (2011) Freeze frame: the Supreme Court's reaffirmation of the substantive principles of preliminary injunctions. Gonzaga Law Rev 47(1):54–98

Goldman JI (2005) Can you freeze assets in a fraudulent conveyance action after Grupo Mexicano? Am Bankr Inst J 54

Jeffrey LW (2005) Three if by equity: Mareva orders & the new British invasion. J Civil Rights and Econ Dev 19(3) Article 5. Available at: http://scholarship.law.stjohns.edu/jcred/vol19/iss3/

Kirschner TJ, Silverman JR (2002) Mareva orders fact or fiction in the United States. Am Bankruptcy Inst J (ABI) (1 Nov 2002 issue), available electronically at http://www.abi.org/abi-journal/mareva-orders-fact-or-fiction-in-the-united-states

Laycock D (1993) The Triumph of Equity. Law & contemporary problems, vol 56, pp 53–82

Park SN (2017) Recognition and enforcement of foreign provisional orders in the United States: toward a practical solution. Univ Pennsylvania J Int Law 38(3):999–1040

Sandrock O (1987) Prejudgment attachments: securing international loans or other claims for money. Int Lawyer 21(1):1–42

Shipley DE (2016) The preliminary injunction standard in diversity: a typical unguided erie choice. Georgia Law Rev 50:1169–1231

Tamaruya M (2010) The Anglo-American perspective on freezing injunctions. Civil Justice Q 29(3):350–368

Wasserman R (1992) Equity renewed: preliminary injunctions to secure potential money judgments. Washington Law Rev 67(1):257–349

Court Cases: United Kingdom

Mareva Compania Naviera SA v International Bulk Carriers SA (the Mareva) (1975) 2 Lloyds Rep. 509 [1980] 1 All ER 213 CA

Court Cases: United States

Allstate Sales and Leasing Co., Inc. v. Geis, 412 N.W.2d 30 (Minn. App., 1987)

Byrd v. Ritchie Grocer Co., decided by Court of Appeals of Arkansas (1985 WL 12622; not reported in S.W.2d [1985])

Civil No. 13 CV 578 (issued on 24th of January 2013 at 1:45 p.m. by US District Court for the Northern District of Illinois, Eastern Division) in the case between the Federal Trade Commission et al. as plaintiffs and Fortune Hi-Tech Marketing Inc. et al. as defendants. See at https://www.ftc.gov/sites/default/files/documents/cases/2013/01/130128fhtmtro.pdf. Accessed 10 Apr 2018

Colman v. Mertes 408 N.W.2d 662 (Minn.App. 1987)

Corporate Commission of the Mille Lacs Band of Ojibwe Indians v. Money Centers of American, Inc. and MCA of Wisconsin, 915 F.Supp.2d 1059 (US District Court D. Minnesota)

Credit Agricole Indosuez v. Rossiyskiy Kredit Bank, 729 N.E.2d 683, 689 (N.Y. 2000)

Fed. Trade Comm'n v. Verity Int'l, 2001 US Dist. LEXIS 6097 (S.D.N.Y. 2001)

FTC v. Fortune Hi-Tech Marketing Inc. et al. Civil No. 13 CV 578 (24th of January 2013) District Court for the Northern District of Illinois, Eastern Division
Fuentes v. Shevin (407 U.S. 67, 92 S. Ct. 1983, 32 L. Ed. 2d 556)
Grupo Mexicano de DeSarrollo, S.A. v. Alliance Bond Fund, Inc. 527 U.S. 308 (1999)
In Re Estate of Ferdinand Marcos, Human Rights Litig., 25 F.3d 1467, 1478 (9th Cir. 1994)
In Re Philip R. Cohn v. David E. Lyon, 11 B.R. 611 (1981)
Mitchell v. W.T. Grant Co., 410 U.S. 600. 94 S. Ct. 1895, 40 L. Ed. 2d 406 (1974)
MS Distrib Co v. Web Records Inc., 2003 US Dist. LEXIS 9092; Philips Med. Sys. Int'l B.V., 8 F.3d (7th Cir. 1993)
MX Distrib Co v. Web Records INc., 2003 US Dist. LEXIS 9092 (N.D. III. 2003)
Perkins v. Quaker City (1956) 165 Ohio St. 120 (Syllabus)
Philips Med. Sys. Int'l B.V., 8 F.3d (7th Cir. 1993)
Prospect Communications v. Herman [2013 WL 6276816] adjudicated by US District Court D. Minnesota (not reported in F.Supp.2d (2013)
Rep. of the Philippines v. Marcos, 862 F2d.1355, 1364 (9th Cir. 1988)
Shipley DE (2016) The preliminary injunction standard in diversity: a typical unguided Erie choice, 50 Ga. L. v. 1169 (2016), at 1171
Sniadach v. Family Finance Corp 395 U.S. 337, 89 S.Ct. 1820, 23 L. Ed. 2d 349 (1969)
State Bank & Trust Company v. Hambone's Corporation, (Court of Common Please, Summit County, Ohio, case No: 2001-11-5455)
III Finance v. Aegis Consumer Funding Group, Inc., 1999 WL 461868 (S.D.N.Y., 1999)

Internet Sources: United States

Uniform Law Commission (2012) The Uniform Asset-Preservation Orders Act—A Symmary

Chapter 4
Post-socialist Jurisdictions: Provisional Measures in Hungary

The law on provisional measures is far from being the same in those countries of the former socialist-block that have acceded to the European Union during the first two decades of the 21st century. We cannot present all of them here, to a great extent because the related English (or other foreign language) literature is extremely scarce and typically limited to description of statutory law. Hungary has been chosen, not just because of language proficiency considerations, but also because Hungarian law represents the conservative end of the spectrum of provisional measure laws. In particular, because it does not know ex parte provisional measures, in stark contrast not only to English, French or US law but also to the laws of some of the countries of the region, like the Czech Republic.[1]

Yet it is far from being irrelevant for any jurisdiction whether its legal system is static and rigid or rather it is increasingly open to understanding the role provisional measures play in the ever-faster moving 21st century characterizes a legal system. The concomitant concern is not only whether courts are willing to award such measures but also whether they are willing to do that with contents that better fit the needs of business life? Hungary unfortunately does not seem to be at the forefront of related developments in the region[2]; as the ensuing discussion will show.

[1] Hergottova (2009), at 160–169.

[2] As opposed to that, at least as Hergottova claimed, "*modestly increasing willingness of the courts to grant interim measures and the more extensive interpretation of courts of the central concept corollary to interim measures—the concept of 'urgent interest' or 'urgent need' [...]*" seems to have been detectable in the Czech Republic already in the first decades of the 21st century. *Id.* at 160.

T. Tajti and P. Iglikowski, *A Cross Border Study of Freezing Orders and Provisional Measures*, SpringerBriefs in Law, https://doi.org/10.1007/978-3-319-94349-7_4

4.1 The Limits of Research: On the Hungarian Legal System and Scholarship

In order to provide the reader with an accurate synopsis of the Hungarian law of provisional measures, it is inevitable to warn the reader about the limits of the ensuing discussion. Especially the following preliminary caveats need to be highlighted.

Firstly, comparative legal scholarship on these procedural devices is very limited in Hungary.[3] In fact, it seem that only one author—Zsuzsa Wopera—ventured as far as taking a look at the Mareva Injunction and other related European and global developments, as well as on their enforceability in Hungary.[4] This is indirect evidence of the low importance attached to provisional relief in Hungary.

Secondly, although the number of reported (publicized) court and various regulatory agency decisions is increasing in Hungary today, only a handful of such case briefs are publicly available that involve provisional measures. Moreover, some of them were made by regulatory agencies (e.g., competition authority). These indirectly prove as well that in Hungary provisional measures are hard to get even in those

---

[3]Admittedly, the number of publications especially from non-English speaking jurisdictions that would have dealt with this query is very limited as well. Though exceptions exist, like the monograph of Weibel (2005), *Enforcement of English Freezing Orders ("Mareva Injunctions") in Switzerland* (Helbing & Lichtenhahn Bruylant, Basel, Bruxelles 2005). (The author argues that Mareva Injunctions would be enforceable in Switzerland based on the Lugano Convention, though "*[as the freezing order is not a final judgment [...] in order to become effective upon enforcement, the order requires, in principle, protective measures under article 39 in addition to the mere declaration of its enforceability.*") *Id.* at 100.

[4]See, e.g., Wopera (2001a, b) [Wopera Brussels Convention 2001], at 743–751. In the article, as Hungary was in process of taking over the *acquie communautaire*—including the Brussels Convention (1968) on jurisdiction and the enforcement of judgments in civil and commercial matters—the author analyzed the compatibility of Hungarian law on provisional measures with European standards. It reviewed the case law of the European Court of Justice (up to 2001) on provisional measures and concluded that Hungarian law satisfies the criteria set by the Court because, first, no independent provisional measure could be asked (i.e., may be asked only linked to a suit) and secondly, a provisional measure could be ordered only after having heard both parties. Id., at 750.

few narrower areas of law (competition/antitrust,[5] trademark[6] and copyright laws[7]) where their ordering was facilitated by the explicit language of sectoral statutes.[8] No empirical evidence or studies are available to suggest the contrary either.

Thirdly, as it will be seen from the ensuing historical review, the law on provisional measures has not changed much since the end of the 19th century, or the beginning of capitalism and the modern era in this country. Perhaps the most critical issue is the lack of ex parte provisional relief,[9] in contrast in particular to the English Mareva Injunction (freezing order) and the French *Saisie Conservatoire*. Obviously, this vacuum represents a major disadvantage of Hungarian law.

Fourthly, as a Continental European civil law system with strong positivistic underpinnings, Hungarian law does not know of *equity* or similar legal tools that would give the courts sufficient flexibility to make 21st century-fitting advancements in the realms of provisional measures law. The tension between business needs and the strict confines of written law, however, are not only felt but sometimes even publicized, as it was with the single reported case in which a first instance court unexpectedly awarded an ex parte measure.[10] As the case was overturned by the

[5]The Hungarian Competition Authority ("*Gazdasági Versenyhivatal*") has issued a modest number of provisional measures in the last few years. Two were against organizers of so-called 'consumer groups' ("*fogyasztói csoport*") prohibiting them to continue publication of their recruitment advertisements (see cases Vj-13/2010 and Vj-18/2010), one was about prohibiting a cable television company from applying its new tariff for year 1999 (see case Vj-175/1998/5), and another one ordering the revocation of a board decision within 15 days (see case Vj-112/2003/27). In yet another case, a provisional measure that was eventually revoked, the Authority prohibited the sale of the marketing of the Noni Tahiti juice (see case Vj 77/2005-12 for the issuance of the measures and decision Vj 177/2004 for its revocation). The texts of the decisions are available in Hungarian language only at the website of the Authority at http://gv.hu. The awarding of provisional measures—similarly to trademarks and copyrights—was incentivized by special provisions added (Section 72A applicable since 1 July 2014) to the 1996 Competition Act ("*1996. évi LVII. Törvény a tisztességtelen piaci magatartás és a versenykorlátozás tilalmáról*").

[6]Section 95 of the Trademark Act of 1997 ("*1997. évi XI. Törvény a védjegyek és a földrajzi árujelzők oltalmáról*") allows issuance of provisional measures against usurpation of trademarks, with the Budapest-Capital Regional Court ("*Fővárosi Törvényszék*") having exclusive jurisdiction, and within six months from the start of usurpation or within sixty days from learning about the usurpation.

[7]Section 94A of the 1999 Copyright Act ("*1999. évi LXXVI. Törvény a szerzői jogról*") contains very similar wording on provisional measures.

[8]The special emphasis attributed to provisional measures in the context of these two areas of intellectual property law were to a great extent due to the TRIPS (Agreement on Trade-Related Aspects of Intellectual Property Rights) and to international obligations taken by Hungary based on related conventions with the EU and the US. See Zsuzsa Wopera (2001) [Wopera History 2001], at 441–43.

[9]Although Wopera's formulation is more cautious, in essence she equally admits that in fact *ex parte* measures are lacking from the Hungarian legal system. As she put it: "[…] *[E]x parte measures could be obtained only in cases of exceptional urgency, a possibility, however, that normally is not existent.*" Wopera (2001a, b) [Wopera History 2001], at 750.

[10]BH2003.110. (Supreme Court decision No.: Legf. Bír. Pf. I/A. 26.945/2001. sz.). The holding of this case clearly supports the claim that Hungarian law has limited ex parte measures to the barest minimum. It states, *first,* that "*the summoning and giving the right to the parties to be heard is not*

Supreme Court, mandating a hearing involving both parties as a precondition for awarding any provisional measure, the decision of the highest Hungarian court in effect was a proclamation of the principle that ex parte measures are *not* recognized in Hungary. In fact, the lack of ex parte provisional measures is undoubtedly that key characteristic of the Hungarian system that primarily justifies classifying it as a conservative system.

Now, let us substantiate the above formulated conclusions in more detail.

4.2 An Overview of the History of Provisional Measures in Hungary in Modern Times (1867—Present Time)

The modern legal history of Hungary is normally divided into three parts, starting with the Austro-Hungarian Compromise of 1867 that denoted also the arrival of capitalism to this part of the world[11] characterized not just by unprecedented economic growth but also by modernization of the legal system involving legal borrowings primarily, but not exclusively,[12] from Germanic systems. The advancement was then stopped by WW I and the subsequent dismemberment of the country, though this early stage-capitalistic development, paralleled by introduction of laws supporting the markets as well, lasted roughly until the end of WW II.

In these years, modernization of the law came to be the rule of the day especially in the last decades of the 19th century. This included the introduction of a modern civil procedure law, the preparations for which began already in 1880 yet were passed only in 1911.[13] From the perspective of our topic, however, of central importance is that in fact this 1911 act did not incorporate provisions on provisional measures that could be obtained rapidly or ex parte. This notwithstanding that the expert, *Kornél Emmer*, who prepared one of the civil procedure code proposals, fiercely tried to persuade the lawmakers on the need for such measures. In fact, he wrote an interesting monograph on the French *référé* system in 1887[14] to promote the cause, not only describing the French idiosyncratic tool in detail but also coming forward with a related model law for Hungary.

required only in exceptionally urgent cases, and if [the properly summoned] party fails to appear at the hearing, or fails to act on a preordered day." *Secondly,* according to the Supreme Court, the first instance court "*should have awarded the provisional measure first by hearing the interested the parties at a joint hearing, and by taking into account the facts that may have changed in the meantime.*"

[11]See, e.g., Kontler (1999), Chapter VI—the Advent of Modernity and the Persistence of the Old Regime (1849–1918) et seq.

[12]On the impact, for example, of Italian law on Hungarian legal system see Tajti (2014a, b), pp. 451–488.

[13]Act of 1911 on Civil Procedure (*1911. évi I. törvénycikk a polgári perrendtartásról*.") See also Zsuzsa Wopera (2001a, b) [Wopera History 2001], at 425–26.

[14]See Emmer (1887). [The Référé-System and its Possible Application in Hungary].

His words deserve to be quoted, not only because they were much ahead of the times he was living in but because the essence remained valid up until today:

> Therefore there are no urgent cases in Hungary? In this country, it is not harmful that instead of immediate protections and remedies, the harmed private right gets recognized [and protected] only in three to six years of successful yet academic litigation, notwithstanding that meanwhile the bad faith party has at its disposal thousands of ways of escaping from under the hands of justice? The damages that good faith parties sustain because of such illegal actions [of bad faith debtors] and the lack of any quick proceedings amount to millions annually […].[15]

Needless to say, the new political system—called 'socialism' by some, and 'communism' by others—imposed after WW II, had different priorities than to introduce major changes in the law on provisional measures. Social peace was more important than the efficient realization of creditors' rights to a society in which ownership and the paraphernalia of capitalism were looked upon with suspicion. As a result, not much has changed in this domain in this period, save that a new Civil Procedure Code was passed in 1952[16] that essentially took over the solutions from the pre-war period. It was not without reason that Wopera, the leading authority on this particular field of law in Hungary concluded that "*[the 1952 Code] in essence took over the earlier (1911 and 1930) solutions […]. [Consequently], the solutions of the 1952 Code were hardly more modern [from the ones in the predecessors.]*"[17]

It is very indicative of the mindset and priorities of those days that the modernization of the law on provision measures did not become topical even in the 1980s, when the 'winds of change' clearly reached the country. As Wopera critically noted, although a series of articles have seen the light in those years arguing for the need to reform the civil procedure law of Hungary, when reading them "*it was conspicuous that none of the authors has raised the issue of the modernization and reform of the legal institution of provisional measures.*"[18] This notwithstanding that there was some governmental support for the reforms.[19] The changes, even if modest compared to the Mareva injunction or the *Saisie Conservatoire*, were rather generated by various international obligations of Hungary, like the ratification of the TRIPS Agreement in 1994[20] that required the signatories to ensure that efficient measures are available to prevent abuse of intellectual property rights.[21] Cases involving provisional measures prohibiting infringement of intellectual property rights, indeed,

---

[15]Emmer (1887), at 48. Quoted also by Wopera (2001a, b), [Wopera History 2001], note 16, at 428.

[16]*A polgári perrendtartásról szóló 1952. évi III. törvény*. [Hereinafter: 1952 Civil Procedure Code].

[17]Wopera (2001a, b), [Wopera History 2001], at 439.

[18]Wopera (2001a, b) [Wopera History 2001], at 440.

[19]The government passed the Decision No. 2024/1980 (XII. 16) foreseeing the comprehensive reform of the 1952 Civil Procedure Code.

[20]The TRIPS Agreement (Agreement on Trade-Related Aspects of Intellectual Property Rights) is an international agreement binding the members of the World Trade Organization (WTO). Hungary ratified it by Parliamentary Decision No. 72/1994 (XII. 27.).

[21]Wopera (2001a, b), [Wopera History 2001], at 441–42.

seem to be among the most frequent ones,[22] though exact quantitative data is not available. In fact, intellectual property rights are subject to a special regime in the Civil Court Enforcement Act resulting in heightened protection.[23]

4.3 Present Time Statutory Law

4.3.1 A Terminology Caveat

The structure of the law on provisional measures and the Hungarian nomenclature does not fit comprehensibly with either English or French law. For this reason, a terminology caveat is due here to avoid misunderstandings. Strictly speaking, Hungarian law, as well as Hungarian legal terminology, makes a strict differentiation between **'interim measures'** (*"ideiglenes intézkedés"*) and **'protective measures'** (*"biztosítási intézkedés"*). While the first is available based on the Civil Procedure Code, the latter is the category regulated by the above mentioned Civil Court Enforcement law. Consequently, while the first aims to provide speedy protective measures during or before litigation (before a final judgment is available), the latter aims to ensure that assets will be available upon which enforcement could be effectuated before all the conditions for issuance of a writ of execution have been fulfilled.[24]

More important is, however, that the effects of the first are *in personam*, and of the latter *in rem*. The first is thus an order to do or not to do something, and the latter essentially a seizure of certain moneys or assets. Consequently, it would be justified to name the first category as *'provisional injunction'* irrespective of the fact that the nature of the measures' effects is not a determinative criterion for Hungarian law. The chosen statutory designations are not reflective of these features of these reliefs either.[25]

However, as the common denominator of both is that they are provisional and they precede the conclusion either of the litigation or enforcement phase, they may conveniently be referred to in this article as *'provisional measures.'* The reader is

---

[22] See, for example, the pretty recent case BH2017.93 involving a request to stop the infringement of the plaintiff's trade mark (concretely: prohibition to engrave on knives marketed by the defendant marks that closely resemble the trade mark the plaintiff lawfully held) within three days and of prohibition of future infringements.

[23] According to § 184/A(3) and (6) of the [Civil] Court Enforcement Act ("1994. *évi LIII. törvény a bírósági végrehajtásról*") the claimant must advance the costs of enforcement of provisional measures to the bailiff. However, once the bailiff has received the moneys, it has to deliver the decree within three days directly to the opponent. If the respondent refuses or fails to perform the bailiff is to turn back to the court for determining the method of enforcement and for imposition of monetary fines.

[24] Oláh and Nagy (2009), pp. 216–315, *in:* Messmann and Tajti (2009).

[25] Note that both devices are in Hungarian named as 'measures' (*"intézkedés"*) and are not differentiated as order (*"utasítás, elrendelés"*) and seizure (*"zárlat"*).

well-advised to pay attention then to whether the discussion is about a measure meted out based on the Civil Procedure Code or civil enforcement law.

4.3.2 The Main Features of the Law on Provisional Measures

The main piece of legislation regulating provisional measures remained the Civil Procedure Code of 1952 even after the change of the regime somewhere around 1990. Although it underwent a major revamping in 1995, the basic stance in relation to and the key rules on provisional measures have not changed. Moreover, one could hardly speak of any revolutionary changes in the brand new Civil Procedure Code that was passed in 2016[26] and which will come into force on the 1st of January 2018[27] either.

The key elements of the law on provisional measures of interest for us—herein solely with reference to the 2016 Civil Procedure Code—would be the following. *First and foremost,* no explicit provision recognizes ex parte measures. The rule is rather that the court must ensure that the opposing party is given the right to be heard,[28] though this right does not mean that the court must always summon a hearing.[29] It seems that the law tries to supplement this deficiency by imposing strict short deadlines on the courts given that courts are to pass a decision on provisional measure requests without delay ("*haladéktalanul*") or maximum within eight days.[30] What the criterion of 'without delay' more concretely means, however, is not clear. No empirical data are available either as to whether this rule means immediate issuance of the order (decree) in the majority of cases. The Code also proclaims that the decree on the provisional measure is enforceable within one day from the delivery of the decree executed in writing.[31]

Secondly, the measures may be issued on four bases by a court decree and always based on a request of a party.[32] These resemble the requirements of the other systems observed herein. These are: (1) preservation of the circumstances that led to the dispute, however, only if restitution later would be impossible (i.e., freezing of the status quo), (2) prohibition of such actions that would prevent the claimant exercising his rights in the future, (3) averting imminent harm or damages, and (4) protection of such rights of the claimant that deserve special appreciation.[33] It is a further restriction that the claimant may not ask for orders requiring such conduct, actions or omissions from the opposing party that may not also be sought in the main proceedings on the

[26] *2016. évi CXXX. Törvény a polgári perrendtartásról.* [Hereinafter: 2016 Civil Procedure Code].
[27] § 630(1) of the 2016 Civil Procedure Code.
[28] § 104(3) of the 2016 Civil Procedure Code.
[29] § 104(4) of the 2016 Civil Procedure Code.
[30] § 104(1) of the 2016 Civil Procedure Code.
[31] § 105(2) of the 2016 Civil Procedure Code.
[32] § 103(1) of the 2016 Civil Procedure Code.
[33] § 103(1) of the 2016 Civil Procedure Code.

merits.[34] As the law provides no further guidance on what such conduct, actions or omissions may be, or concretely what the contents of the provisional measures could be, the reported cases, at least theoretically, may be resorted to.

Thirdly, the relevant provisions of the 2016 Hungarian Civil Procedure Code, similarly to the other jurisdictions within the purview of this article, evidence that the system is equally concerned with maintaining a proper balance between the parties. The basic principle thus proclaims that the court decision on provisional measures must always ensure "*that the measure would not be more detrimental to the opposing party—taking into account the potential duty to provide security—than the refusal to award the measure to the claimant*."[35] Furthermore, the decree awarding the provisional measure is appealable,[36] is of limited duration,[37] and the court may request provision of security. The court is to ask for counter security if the opposing party proves that the provisional measure would inflict upon him such harm, damages or disadvantages that would entitle him to claim damages in the case of the claimant losing the case on the merits.[38]

4.4 What Contemporary Hungarian Court Cases Can Tell Us About Ex Parte and Other Provisional Measures

4.4.1 Case Law as a Source for Analysis: Limitations and Key Features

Hungary is a civil law country, where the primary sources of law are codes and statutory law. This notwithstanding, the importance of court cases and Supreme Court positions[39] is increasing in Hungary as well, similarly not just to the major European civilian jurisdictions but also as for the neighbors of Hungary. This is a

[34] § 103(2) of the 2016 Civil Procedure Code.

[35] § 104(2) of the 2016 Civil Procedure Code.

[36] § 105(1) of the 2016 Civil Procedure Code.

[37] § 103(2) of the 2016 Civil Procedure Code.

[38] As per § 105(4) of the 2016 Civil Procedure Code, unless revoked by a court decision earlier, the provisional measure remains in force until the finality of the first instance judgment brought on the merits.

[39] Perhaps the most important recent development in Hungary as far as the position and role as a source of law of court decisions is concerned relates to the new tasks of the Hungarian Supreme Court named the Curia ("*Kúria*"). Namely, as per article 25(3) of the Basic Law (i.e., constitution) of Hungary enacted in 2011, Curia was entrusted with passing so-called 'unifying decisions' that have binding force on courts. As the Basic Law formulated: "the Curia shall ensure uniformity of the application of the law by the courts and shall take uniformity decisions which shall be binding on the courts." Besides these the various Departments ("*Kollégium*") of the Curia make as well Opinions on various legal issues, which—although not having a constitution-based binding force—have not only persuasive force but are applied whenever a case reaches the Curia. See, e.g., Lábady (2013), at 137.

major change because reported court- and other classes of cases[40] bring to the surface empirical evidence, which may be invaluable in the context of such legal devices as provisional measures, where the law provides some flexibility and gives discretion to courts on the basis of which ingenious lawyers could shape the contents of the measures and judges seek to satisfy genuine business needs. Put simply, it is the cases that reveal with considerable certainty what are the kinds of measures sought by parties as well as their contents.

Another limitation of the present Hungarian case reporting system of utmost relevance to our subject matter is that the focus unwittingly is only on substantive law and not on the enforceability of the provisional measures awarded. What one could learn is only whether a provisional measure with a certain content is recognized by the courts and thus whether they could be sought by parties, however, no evidence, or empirical analyses could be found on whether such measures are readily enforceable and "have teeth" in real life? While it is generally considered that the Mareva (freezing) Injunction works in practice, perhaps primarily because of the severe contempt of court rules, this is something not determinable in Hungary with sufficient precision. This caveat should therefore be borne in mind when considering the ensuing case briefs, the review of which inevitably will focus on non-ex parte measures given that Hungarian law does not know ex parte provisional measures.

4.4.2 Why a Mareva Injunction-Type Ex Parte Provisional Measure Is Needed in Hungary?

If juxtaposed to the Mareva Injunction and especially the useful practical goals the Mareva has successfully served since its inception, it is hard not to conclude—similarly to the 19th century commentator *Kornél Emmer* mentioned above—that there may be valid practical reasons for which this type of measure would be needed in Hungary as well. This can be corroborated also by two cases of pretty recent vintage, which notwithstanding the small number of reported cases on the topic may be instructive and persuasive.

The text of the Basic Law in English is available electronically at http://www.kormany.hu/download/e/02/00000/The%20New%20Fundamental%20Law%20of%20Hungary.pdf. [Accessed on 15 Apr. 2018].

See also the article of Ződi (2014), *Precedenskövetés és Jogszabályértelmezés* (Following Precedents and Interpretation of Law), in which he argues that although Hungarian law is not a 'precedents-based legal system,' there are some similarities with how higher courts work in common law systems. Paper available through the website of the Institute for Legal Studies of the Hungarian Academy of Sciences at http://jog.tk.mta.hu/uploads/files/Allam-%20es%20Jogtudomany/2014_3/2014-3-beliv-ZODI.pdf. [Accessed on 15 Apr. 2018].

[40] For example, public procurement committees ("*közbeszerzési döntőbizottság*") have discretionary powers also to issue provisional measures. See EBH2004.1091.

The first case was already mentioned above[41] because it is the only single traceable reported court case in which a court (concretely the first instance court) did issue an ex parte provisional measure notwithstanding the lack of any explicit statutory background. The judge obviously found it important to meet the exigencies of the facts and circumstances of the case by granting relief without giving a chance to the opposing party to be heard. In other words, the case evidences that, indeed, there are situations in which ex parte provisional measures are the right solutions. As the Supreme Court was of a contrary opinion and overturned the first instance decision, the case properly illustrates as well how deep the conflict between practical needs and theoretical presumptions are, especially if the latter are assumed uncritically.

The *second case*[42] deserves attention not because the judge awarded either an ex parte or some unusual provisional measure. It is rather the factual matrix involved that makes the case interesting. Namely, the facts of the case closely resemble the circumstances for which the Mareva Injunction was initially conceived in the United Kingdom. Concretely, a gas development-related service contract was at stake, the implementation of which turned sour when one of the gas wells exploded causing significant environmental damage presumably due to fault of the service-provider. The principal (claimant) initiated arbitration proceedings and parallel with that asked for both protective measures (seizing of certain assets of the respondent) and provisional injunctions (prohibition of sale or encumbering of certain immovables). These measures were requested because there was evidence that the respondent had taken steps to close down its business in Hungary and move its assets out of the country. Moreover, the Hungarian Mining Authority determined that such damages were caused by the respondent.

Although the publicized case brief fails to reveal all details, it seems that the requests for the measures were justified as they did not rest solely on pure allegations of the claimant. Irrespective of that the measures were not issued by the court. What is striking is that the key issue discussed by all the different courts at each respective level was solely about distinguishing provisional injunctions from preventive measures. The gist of the holding is that while provisional injunctions—as formulated by the first instance court and approved by the Supreme court—"*cannot restrict the ownership rights of the respondent in order to secure the enforcement of [a] damage claim,*"[43] protective measures could not be awarded in the case because "*the existence, amount and maturity of the [damages] claim*" was not yet determined by a public document or by a private document with full probative force.[44]

Therefore, as one could conclude, formalism prevailed in the case and even these quoted fragments may properly show how deeply positivistic thinking is engraved in Hungarian lawyers. This notwithstanding that there are judges who realize—as illustrated by the first case—how grave the dissonance between statutory law and

[41]BH2003.110. See Section 3.2. and the concomitant notes in this part on Hungarian law above.

[42]BH2002.441 (Legf. Bír. Pf. I/A. 26.108/2001). For brief description and critical analysis of the case see Messmann and Tajti (2009), volume I, at 249–257.

[43]Id. at 255.

[44]Id. at 255.

business needs occasionally is. The court's perception of what a court may order—or what an injunction as an order prohibiting someone to do or not to do something is about—deserves comment as well. This because in the interpretation of the court, prohibition to remove assets out of the jurisdiction would amount to such a '*restriction of ownership rights*' that the law cannot tolerate. Put simply, while freezing of assets through ordering the defendant not to remove his assets out of the jurisdictions is the gist of the Mareva Injunction, it is something inappropriate under Hungarian law. This train of thought must have been a misunderstanding on the side of the Hungarian first instance court given that an order prohibiting disposal of an asset is clearly not the equivalent of a seizure (arrest) of an asset—even as per Hungarian law.

4.4.3 *What Are* Non-*Ex Parte Provisional Measures Used for in Hungary?*

The picture is more varied, however, when non-ex parte provisional measures are at stake in Hungary. As these may also be telling about the flexibility and the business-friendliness of the system, a brief account of a selected number of reported cases should be welcome. It makes sense, however, to take a look here only at reported cases from the post-1990 era, starting with the transition to democracy and a market economy, leading to accession to the European Union in 2004. This because the increased impact of globalization, EU and foreign law, as well as western business practices, the understanding of market economy institutions has increased considerably in Hungary in the past two decades and half. This is visible even from the ensuing few case briefs notwithstanding that only some of the cases evidence traces of legal engineering and most of them bring to the surface rather classical issues and solutions. Reading the case briefs one should keep in mind that the these cases contain the best empirical, though indirect, evidence on what provisional measures could be obtained today in Hungarian courts and what would be their likely contents. The common denominator of all the cases discussed, however, is that that none of them possesses the most valuable feature of either *Mareva* or *Saisie*: the surprise effect.[45]

One case from 2008,[46] presumably the most complex reported case involving provisional measures, leaves the impression that even the basic features and effects of provisional measures may be obscure. The case is illustrative of the conflict of a security interest (constructive pledge) and a preliminary injunction, or the conflict of *in rem* and *in personam* rights, given that the central issue was whether the court

[45] As Hoyle put it in his treatise on freezing and search orders: "*Speed is required in applying for a Freezing Order to maintain the element of surprise. A without notice application is therefore vital, as it is hardly consistent with the fear of a defendant dissipating his assets if not restrained, to give him advance notice of the hearing.*" Hoyle 2006, para 1.22, at 8. As a justification he then add that the number of applications to discharge Freezing Orders is '*comparatively rare.*' *Id.*

[46] BH2008.93.

may issue a provisional measure ordering transfer of possession on certain goods (488.940, liters of Tokay wine) pledged and in the hands of a field warehousing company.[47] The case—lasting for about five years—went through three instances and was then dropped back for new proceedings, before the Hungarian Supreme Court could finally adjudicate that the warehouse must hand over the possession over the collateral in its hands to no one else but to the presenter of the warehouse receipts that represented the goods in question. In other words, a court may not issue a provisional measure for the benefit of a creditor who is not the rightful holder of the said warehouse receipts. The strange twist in the case, illustrating that not only the courts but businessmen (and their counsel) as well do not necessarily understand the law on provisional measures or secured transactions law, is that the warehouse was willing to transfer possession of the wines notwithstanding that they were used as collateral securing the claims of a third party creditor and without having ensured that such creditor's rights were first paid.

In a 2003 case,[48] based on a similarly complex factual matrix, the issue was whether the court can issue a provisional measure ordering the deletion of an entry from the real property (immovables) registry? The complexity of the case was due to the fact that the entry on acquisition of title on certain immovables was through exercise of the option to acquire title on the immovables in question. The option right was initially given as a security to one of the partners, who provided financing for a joint venture aimed at developing, renting and otherwise exploiting certain immovables. Once the business turned sour, the financier exercised its option and the registry duly entered his acquisition of title (ownership) into the books. As a response, the other party launched a suit asking for annulment of the option contract and parallel with that the deletion of the title acquired by the exercise of the option. According to the Supreme Court's holding, the entry from the registry books may be deleted only if first the option rights contract is invalidated something which, however, would require passing of a decision on the merits of the claim. In brief, the deletion of a purchase right (acquisition of title) may not be ordered by a provisional measure.

In a case reported on no more than a page,[49] the issue was whether a money-freezing order can be issued to secure payment of future harm. Namely, as per the

[47]Presently in Hungary two types of warehouses are in widespread use: the public (terminal) and field (or artificial) warehouses. While the first are the paradigm warehousing forms known all over the world, variants of field (artificial) warehouses are peculiarities only of a few legal systems. The key differences between the two is that while in case of public warehouses (which are typically located in industrial centers) it is the debtor (e.g., a farmer or producer of canned products) who transports his goods to the warehouse, in case of field warehouses it is the warehousing company that goes to the premises of the debtor, where it erects an 'artificial' warehouse. Consequently, in case of field warehouses the debtor does not have to transports his goods. If the warehoused goods are meant to be processed, they would be in such case close to the production line of the debtor. While field warehousing was a major business form and security device in the United States roughly until the 1960s, they became (in somewhat different form than in the US) extremely popular in Hungary roughly in the 21st century. See Tajti T. (2014), [Field Warehousing], at 185–235.

[48]BH2003.337.

[49]BH2002.315.

reasoning of the claimants, if they would be paid only after having won the case and not immediately, their health would be seriously damaged in the meantime as they would not be in the position to pay the increased healthcare costs. In the opinion of the court awarding of such a provisional measure is not possible because that would amount to adjudicating the merits. If appropriately proven, however, a provisional order could be ordered for *imminent* harm or damages (“*fenyegető kár*”). Yet even in that case the provisional measure would be justified only if the harm or damages would be caused by repeated wrongful acts, or continuation of a wrongful situation (“*jogellenes magatartás ismétlése vagy a jogellenes helyzet fennmaradása*”) and if the measure would prohibit such actions or would put an end to such circumstances—but it could not under any circumstances amount to damages (“*kártérítés*”).

In a labor law case from 2016[50] that also involved a request for a provisional measure that would order the defendant—the employer—to pay a relatively high amount of money (five million HUF)[51] before adjudication of the claim, the high court found the request justified, however, it awarded only a quarter of the requested amount. It was of relevance that the merits of the case concerned compensation for a workplace accident that decreased the claimant's capacity for work. Interestingly, the first instance court initially rejected the request because it found that the amount of damages that were to be paid by the employer was very uncertain.

In another case from 2000,[52] concerning wrongful sub-licensing of television broadcasting rights, a two-prong provisional measure was awarded by the court. While, on one hand, it prohibited the licensee (first defendant) from sub-licensing, on the other hand, it also prohibited the second defendant from effecting any television broadcasting on local soccer league matches in any form without permission of the plaintiff-licensor. Interestingly, the second provisional measure was awarded with *immediate effect.*

That businessmen and their counsel may be capable of finding innovative solutions in Hungary as well is properly illustrated by a recent case trying to halt the enforcement of a controversial tobacco regulation from 2014 making sale of tobacco products subject to governmental licensing and in effect leading to redistribution of the market.[53] One of the measures introduced by the law, for example, was redistribution of the licenses, with old shops losing their share of the market, and new participants getting profitable monopolies. As far as the merits of the case are concerned, the court was asked to declare that the said regulatory regime does not apply to the claimant. At the same time, the court was petitioned to issue a provisional measure that would prohibit the competent licensing governmental body to issue any license, or conclude any contract or take any other measure with third persons affecting the tobacco market of the claimant. The claim was rejected on the grounds

[50]EBD2016.M18.

[51]The exchange rate of the Hungarian Forint (HUF) in the first half of 2017 fluctuated between 303 to 316 HUF for a Euro. Thus, five million HUF would be around 16,000 Euros.

[52]BH2000.406.

[53]BH2016.339.

that it had no valid legal basis and parallel with that the request for the said provisional measure as well. As the Supreme Court said: "[…] *while the government may be sued for the harm and damages caused by the lawmaker, the determination of whether a particular law applies to the plaintiffs may not be the subject of a suit before a court of law.*"[54]

4.5 Contempt of Court Rules in Hungary

As we have seen above, not only the Mareva Injunction but also the US TROs and preliminary injunctions work efficiently to a great extent due to the stiff contempt of court rules, which courts additionally do not loathe to apply if need be. Moreover, while these Anglo-Saxon systems have comprehensive contempt of court laws, one would have difficulty to locate the equivalent in Hungarian law because the latter has nothing more than a few provisions scattered around the Civil Procedure Act and the various distinct acts each regulating one specific type of court procedure. From a formal point of view thus only these scarce provisions scattered around more statutes could be pointed at as the ones that common law lawyers would perceive as 'contempt of court rules.' This notwithstanding that the Criminal Code also recognises a few crimes that aim to protect courts. In this respect, therefore, Hungarian law's approach is very similar to the French one sketched above.

Unfortunately, the Civil Procedure Act 2016 fails to specifically address what happens if provisional measures (injunctions) are willingly disobeyed, which is indirectly a proof of our earlier point that in Hungary provisional remedies are largely neglected topics. True, the act foresees that fines (as limited by law)[55] may be imposed for some explicitly listed disrespects of the law and the court, like filing of baseless claims,[56] inappropriate behavior in the court room,[57] or not acting in good faith,[58] yet these could hardly be applied for breach of preliminary injunctions by analogy or otherwise. The Civil Court Enforcement statute[59] provides for somewhat more precise and stiffer rules. Suffice to mention here that based on the main related section, a disciplinary penalty may be imposed on the debtor and others for disobeying enforcement orders or for hindering the enforcement procedure otherwise.

Given the lack of empirical evidence, however, it is hard to tell whether these have "teeth" in reality. As opposed to either England or the US, where it is commonly

---

[54] Id.

[55] As per Section 52 of the Civil Procedure Act 2016, the maximum monetary fines are one-million HUF, which in case of minors may not exceed three-hundred-thousand HUF. These may not be changed to prison based on explicit provision of the Act and in principle the value of fine may not exceed the value of the claim either (Section 52(2)).

[56] § 219 of the Civil Procedure Act 2016.

[57] § 236 of the Civil Procedure Act 2016.

[58] § 5(2) of the Civil Procedure Act 2016.

[59] Act No. LIII. of 1994 on Civil Court Enforcement (as amended) (*1994. évi LIII. törvény a bírósági végrehajtásról*).

known that contempt of court rules are the token of efficiency of the respective provisional measures, such a clearly identifiable contingency, neither exists, nor is spoken of in Hungary for the time being.

4.6 Positioning Hungarian Law on the European and Global Landscape

Based on the above, contemporary Hungarian law on provisional measures should undoubtedly be placed among the more conservative legal systems. The two main reasons being, *first,* the lack of ex parte measures, and *second*, the relative unpredictability of the system as a result of which it is hard to obtain provisional measures from courts. Moreover, courts are reluctant to order measures with novel, unorthodox contents, corresponding to what the ever-newer circumstances brought forward by the necessities of the 21st century often would require. No scholarly publication seems to have seen the daylight yet that would have proven, or at least would have claimed the contrary.

Undoubtedly a handful of reasons could be listed to explain such a state of affairs, from lack of tradition, dominance of positivism through to the defects of statutory drafting. As one source suggested on the limits of written law, one of the reasons that provisional measures are hard to obtain may rest with the "... *rather general wording of the Civil Procedure Act on provisional injunctions [because of why] Hungarian courts are reluctant to grant this measure [fearing] that their order will be annulled by the second instance court*."[60] Although this claim was made in relation to the Civil Procedure Code 1952, nothing indicates that things will improve under the new Code to step in to force on the 1st of January 2018.

There is thus, a stark contrast between Hungary as compared especially to France and England (and partly also vis-à-vis the US). This because—as opposed to Hungary—in the latter two jurisdictions, in the opinion of both academic writers and practitioners freezing orders and the *Saisie Conservatoire* respectively are readily available, can realistically be obtained if the preconditions are fulfilled and the pertaining law is predictable. If Hungarians would be asked the same questions, however, their responses would not necessarily match what has been said of the availability of provisional measures.

These features of Hungarian law on provisional measures make it the most conservative of all the observed systems herein. In the light of the above, Hungarian scholars and policy-makers should be persuaded to give more closer consideration to the consequences on business and other related social issues such a stance has.

[60] Messmann and Tajti (2009), at 251.

References

EU Legislation

Brussels Convention (1968) On jurisdiction and the enforcement of judgments in civil and commercial matters (Official Journal L 299, 31/12/1972 P. 0032–0042)

Hungarian Law

Act of 1911 on Civil Procedure (1911. évi I. törvénycikk a polgári perrendtartásról")
[Civil] Court Enforcement Act of 1994 ("1994. évi LIII. törvény a bírósági végrehajtásról")
Civil Procedure Code of 1952 ("A polgári perrendtartásról szóló 1952. évi III. Törvény")
Civil Procedure Code of 2016 (2016. évi CXXX. Törvény a polgári perrendtartásról
Competition Act of 1996 ("1996. évi LVII. törvény a tisztességtelen piaci magatartás és a versenykorlátozás tilalmáról")
Copyright Act of 1999 ("1999. évi LXXVI. törvény a szerzői jogról")
[Governmental] Decision No. 2024/1980 (XII. 16) foreseeing the comprehensive reform of the 1952 Civil Procedure Code
Trademark Act of 1997 ("1997. évi XI. törvény a védjegyek és a földrajzi árujelzők oltalmáról")

International Law

World Trade Organization (WTO), TRIPS Agreement (Agreement on Trade-Related Aspects of Intellectual Property Rights). The TRIPS Agreement is Annex 1C of the Marrakesh Agreement Establishing the World Trade Organization, signed in Marrakesh, Morocco on 15 Apr 1994

Books: In English Language

Hergottova A (2009) Enforcement of contracts in the Czech Republic. In: Messmann S, Tajti T (eds) The case law of Central and Eastern Europe—Enforcement of Contracts, vol I. European University Press, Bochum-Germany
Hoyle MSW (2006) Freezing and search orders, 4th edn. Informa-London
Kontler L (1999) Millennium in Central Europe—A history of Hungary. Atlantisz Publishing House, Budapest
Messmann S, Tajti T (2009) The case law of Central and Eastern Europe—Enforcement of Contracts. European University Press, Bochum-Germany
Oláh Zs. and Nagy I. Cs. (2009), Enforcement of Contracts in Hungary, in: Messmann S. & Tajti T., the Case Law of Central and Eastern Europe - Enforcement of Contracts, vol. I. European University Press, Bochum-Germany
Weibel T (2005) Enforcement of English freezing orders ("Mareva Injunctions") in Switzerland. Helbing & Lichtenhahn Bruylant, Basel-Bruxelles

Books: In Hungarian Language

Emmer K (1887) A Référé-rendszer s magyar alkalmazása [The Référé-System and its [Possible] Application in Hungary]. Franklin Társulat, Budapest

Lábady T (2013) A magánjog általános tana. Szent István Társulat, Budapest

Articles: In English Language

Tajti T (2014) Italian law in Hungary. In: Bussani M (eds) Il Diritto Italiano in Europa (1861–2014)—Scienza, giurisprudenza, legislazione, Edition: Anno 2014, vol V. Edizioni Scientifiche Italiana

Tajti T (2014) The resurrection of fields warehousing—the Booming Hungarian field warehousing sector, the incomplete english narrative and the Unexplored field warehousing law of the United States, Acta Juridica Hungarica 55(3):185–235. [Referred to as: Field Warehousing]

Articles: In Hungarian Language

Ződi Zs (2014) Precedenskövetés és Jogszabályértelmezés (Following/Adherence to Precedents and Interpretation of Law). In the Hungarian language law review Állam és Jogtudomány vol LX, No 3, pp 60–85

Wopera Zs (2001) Az ideiglenes intézkedések a Brüsszeli Egyezmény 24. cikkére vonatkozó európai bírósági joggyarkorlat tükrében. Magyar Jog, vol 2001, No 12, pp 743–751. [Referred to as: Wopera Brussels Convention 2001]

Wopera Zs (2001) Az ideiglenes intézkedés szabályozásának története Magyarországon 1868-tól a polgári perrendtartás VI. Novellájának megalkotásáig. Section Juridica et Politica, Miskolc, Tomus XIX, pp 423–444 [Referred to as: Wopera History 2001]

Court and Administrative Agency Cases: Hungary

Hungarian Compatition Authority
Vj-175/1998/5
Vj-112/2003/27
Vj-13/2010
Vj-18/2010)
Vj 77/2005-12

Court and administrative agency cases: Courts

BH2000.406
BH2002.441 (Legf. Bír. Pf. I/A. 26.108/2001)
BH2002.315

BH2003.337
BH2003.110. (Supreme Court decision No.: Legf. Bír. Pf. I/A. 26.945/2001)
EBH2004.1091
BH2008.93
EBD2016.M18
BH2016.339
BH2017.93

Chapter 5
The European Account Preservation Order: Nuclear Weapon or Paper Tiger?

Proper assessment of the utility of the Mareva Injunction and the *Saisie Conservatoire* would not be possible without casting a few words on one of the most recent European developments: the availability of the European Account Preservation Order (hereinafter: EAPO) since 18 January 2017 when Regulation 655/2014—that created it—came into being.[1] As this is a brand new development, empirical evidence does not exist as of yet and hence one has no other option but to base our comments solely on the black letters of the Regulation as supplemented by the accompanying publications of the European Commission (or the bodies having worked under the auspices of the Commission)[2] and the comments of affected industries rather than referring to case law or the works of scholars.[3]

As far as the opinions of international law firms are concerned, a random look at the already available internet-based publications suggests that the pessimistic views seem to dominate. Very illustrative of the negative position is the 2014 Briefing Note of Clifford Chance foretelling that "*the Regulation could well join the club of largely unused EU civil justice measures.*"[4] Unfortunately, there may be a lot of truth in this sinister qualification as it is next to natural that the original ideas in the EU lawmaking process are normally significantly altered, making out of an originally powerful legal device only a weak shadow by the end of the process. Additionally,

---

[1] Section 54 of Regulation 655/2014 of the European Parliament and of the Council of 15 May 2014 establishing a European Account Preservation Order procedure to facilitate cross-border debt recovery in civil and commercial matters.

[2] For a succinct overview of the procedures for the issuance and enforcement of EAPOs see European Commission, *Judicial Cooperation in Civil Matters in the European Union—A Guide for Legal Practitioners* (2014), at 105–109.

[3] EAPOs have so far largely escaped the attention of scholars though shorter papers with some critical points are available. See, e.g., Owens (16 Oct. 2016) and Kyriakides (2014). [Both accessed 15 April 2018].

[4] See Carty and James (Sept. 2014). For a somewhat more optimistic comment see the recent comments of the Vienna-based law firm Schönherr from under the pen of Simss and Lehfuss (2017), [Both accessed 15 Apr. 2018].

T. Tajti and P. Iglikowski, *A Cross Border Study of Freezing Orders and Provisional Measures*, SpringerBriefs in Law, https://doi.org/10.1007/978-3-319-94349-7_5

the meaningfully differing implementation of EU legislation by the Member States just further complicates things.

Still, until instructive empirical evidence in sufficient quantity will be available, the thoughts that follow are essentially speculative. This notwithstanding, we could already predict with some accuracy that EAPOs may inevitably affect Mareva Injunctions and Freezing Orders as well as *Saisie Conservatoires* in radically different ways.

The verdict on the relationship of the Mareva Injunction and the Freezing Order as to the EAPO is easier to pass. It is not only that the UK has opted out of the Regulation[5] when passed but following the 2016 UK referendum vote and the UK's withdrawal from the EU (Brexit) this makes the question partly superfluous and partly contingent on the results of the EU-UK negotiations. Perhaps most contentious is whether UK courts will be in the position to issue EAPOs, though it is unclear at the moment as well whether it will be possible to freeze assets in the UK by resorting to EAPOs issued in an EU Member State. EAPOs remain, however, of interest to UK companies having affiliations in the EU. The aggregate result of all this is that the importance of the Mareva Injunctions will most likely remain unscathed by these developments in the EU. Finally it should be noted that the EAPO is not available for arbitration which is excluded from the areas of law to which it can apply. Many international commercial agreements have arbitration clauses so this will be a severely limiting factor and consequently the EAPO is less likely to affect the popularity of the Mareva Injunction for this reason as well.

It is less easy to make exact projections on whether the EAPOs are going to tarnish the fame of *Saisie Conservatoires* given that France has neither opted out of the Regulation nor is in the process of leaving the EU. To address this query two sets of issues need to be looked at. These we could conveniently refer to as formal and empirical factors.

As far as the formal side of the question is concerned, it is sufficient to juxtapose the known key differences of the two devices to realize that the EAPO was not designed to become a full substitute of the French freezing order. The EU Commission itself launched it as "*an alternative to instruments existing under national law*."[6] Besides the fact that this device is available only in cross-border cases involving "*pecuniary claims in civil and commercial matters*"[7] and can be employed only on bank accounts of a debtor, the Regulation narrows down the reach of the device by adding express exclusions. In particular, it cannot be employed in arbitration, insolvency and proceedings involving wills and successions.[8] For each of the exempted instances therefore the *Saisie* should be resorted to if compatible at all.

Apart from these formal considerations, it remains to be seen as well what the attitude of national courts will be and whether the Regulation will be enforced as

[5]See para 50 of Regulation 655/2014.

[6]European Commission communication '*Preservation of Bank Accounts*' available electronically at http://ec.europa.eu/justice/civil/commercial/freeze-accounts/index_en.htm. [Accessed 15 April 2018].

[7]Article 2(1) of the Regulation.

[8]Article 2(2) of the Regulation.

smoothly and efficiently as foreseen by its provisions?[9] Questions along the lines of an established versus a new, untested device, as well as the local versus foreign procedural device undoubtedly arise. In case of such procedural devices as EAPOs concretely national civil procedure law is "*the vehicle that transports EU law*" and therefore the national courts are the ones that should ensure that "*the exercise of EU rights [is not] made virtually impossible or excessively difficult*."[10]

Last but not least, although it may not be apposite to go as far as mentioning the impact of potential abuses yet they should also be reckoned with when assessing the potential success of EAPO. Obviously only the empirical evidence to emerge could tell as to which side the balance is going to tilt in the years to come. What should, however, be beyond doubt is that the French *Saisie Conservatoire*, and its related legal measures in other EU Member States, hardly will become redundant because of the introduction of European EAPOs. Apart from the internet articles from law firms mentioned above there is, for example, very little evidence of the EAPO attracting interest in France. This may be because it only entered into force in January 2017. Leaving aside inevitable conservatism in the legal community it could also be suggested that practitioners would prefer to concentrate on taking measures before their local courts rather than venturing to seek provisional legal steps which are enforceable in other EU member states. From a practical perspective any creditor seeking to make use of the EAPO would almost certainly require assistance from qualified lawyers in his own EU member state as well as any EU member state which holds bank accounts which could be attached. This may perhaps make the new device less attractive as an alternative option to steps before the local courts because the creditor may find he becomes involved in two sets of different legal proceedings in two different EU states with consequent exposure to increased costs.

---

[9]In particular the following should make EAPOs efficient. *First and foremost*, they are issued by courts *ex parte* (Art. 11) and within short deadlines (Art. 18). While in this first phase the rules admittedly are straightforward, one should not forget that the courts asked to issue EAPOs have some discretion as well. It remains to be seen whether *ex parte* measures are compatible with such legal systems as Hungary that do not provide for issuance of provisional measures without notice and opportunity to be heard. *For* example, courts—if allowed by the laws of the Member State having jurisdiction to issue the order and if the court is of the opinion that the evidence provided by the applicant is insufficient—may ask for additional evidence from the applicant (Art 9(1)), what may prolong the proceedings. *Secondly,* in the second phase, where the already issued Preservation Order needs to be enforced in such another Member States where the debtor has bank accounts, rules exist as well to ensure efficiency. For example, there is no need to obtain a declaration of enforceability (Art. 22) and all authorities handling the case are expected to act without delay (Art. 23(2)). While this may in principle ensure maximum speed of action, given that the further steps are to be undertaken exactly as for "*equivalent national orders*" (Art. 23(1)), if this prong does not work properly in a jurisdiction in general, that may slow down the process of enforcement of EAPOs.

[10]See Krans (2015), at 572. (Defining the 'invisible pillar' as "*European influence on national civil procedure*" and as a factor that leads to increased Europeanization of procedural laws and arguing that this leads to differences in the application of European laws by various Member States and within the Member states—to wit, external and internal fragmentation). *Id.* at 587.

References

EU Legislation

Regulation 655/2014 of the European Parliament and of the Council of 15 May 2014 establishing a European Account Prevention Order procedure to facilitate cross-border debt recovery in civil and commercial matters

EU Soft Law

European Commission, Judicial Cooperation in Civil Matters in the European Union—A Guide for Legal Practitioners (2014)

Articles

Krans B (2015) EU law and national civil procedure law: An invisible pillar. Eur Rev Private Law 23(4–2015):567–588

Kyriakides N (2014) The United Kingdom's stance to recently introduced European account preservation order. Civil Justice Q 33(4):375–378

Owens A (2016) Analysis of the requirements for the grant of a European account preservation order. Glasgow University Law Rev (Electron J). Available electronically at http://www.gulawreview.org/entries/commercial/analysis-of-the-requirements-for-the-grant-of-a-european-account-preservation-order

Internet Sources

European Commission Communication (2014) Preservation of bank accounts. Available electronically at European Commission communication 'Preservation of Bank Accounts' available electronically at http://ec.europa.eu/justice/civil/commercial/freeze-accounts/index_en.htm. Accessed 10 June 2018.

Simss M, Lehfuss N (2017) Freeze! Securing a debtor's assets in a foreign country cab be a difficult and lengthy exercise—a new EU regulation will change that. Available at http://www.schoenherr.eu/publications/publications-detail/freeze-securing-a-debtors-assets-in-a-foreign-country-can-be-a-difficult-and-lengthy-exercise-a/

Chapter 6
Conclusions and Possible Ways Forward

This article has examined the provisional measures relating to freezing assets of two major common law jurisdictions and two important civil law systems. The authors were in particular guided by the cautionary words of the concurring and dissenting Justices of the US Supreme Court in the 1999 *Grupo Mexicano* case according to which the "*age of slow-moving capital and comparatively immobile wealth*" is bygone. This is a change that has inevitably increased the importance of provisional measures as well. While the validity of this train of thought might have been questioned in 1999, it could hardly be doubted anymore now close to the end of the second decade of the 21st century.

Therefore the authors can tentatively reach the following conclusions about the respective features and advantages of the available remedies examined.

As far as the United Kingdom is concerned, the Mareva Injunction is promoted by English lawyers as the most advanced and effective procedure available to preserve assets for an unpaid creditor before judgment. Since its introduction forty years ago it has been developed expanded and improved by a substantial volume of case law. In particular it allows a creditor to obtain orders affecting the assets of his debtor worldwide. Something which no other legal system can achieve by comparison. The Freezing Order has been adopted with enthusiasm by the United Kingdom's many former colonies with success. And some of these jurisdictions, notably Singapore, pose an increasing threat by way of competition to London in the international sphere. Consequently, it should not come as a surprise that the Mareva and the ancillary Search Order (initially Anton Pillar Order) are now increasingly on the international scene epitomized as the '*nuclear weapons of the law*.'

But the criticism which is frequently levelled at the English Freezing Order is its cost and complexity in comparison with other notably civil law pre judgment remedies. It is undeniable that potential litigants will only resort to Freezing Orders and the Commercial Court in London if the amounts involved are very substantial. And the risks of exposure to financial sanctions (including legal costs to be paid to opponents as well as damages) are equally significant for a creditor.

T. Tajti and P. Iglikowski, *A Cross Border Study of Freezing Orders and Provisional Measures*, SpringerBriefs in Law, https://doi.org/10.1007/978-3-319-94349-7_6

Since the United Kingdom's decision to leave the EU, English lawyers have been very wary to maintain London's pre-eminent status in international litigation in the post Brexit era. The United Kingdom's European competitors are well aware of that and eager to take any opportunity for a bigger market share for legal services. The principal criticism of the English legal system is invariably its expense and complexity in comparison to other systems. English law is highly regarded and frequently chosen as applicable law in international contracts. But there is an increasing tendency to apply English law to a contract but avoid London as a centre for dispute resolution whether for arbitration or the civil courts.

The French *Saisie Conservatoire* compares very favourably with the English Freezing order on many fronts. It is much less expensive. It is much less complicated and easier to obtain in practice. It exposes the creditor to relatively little in terms of a risk of being found liable to his opposing party for legal costs or damages for an arrest which is subsequently set aside. The French *Saisie Conservatoire* has the further advantage that—given its *in rem* effect—it can create preferential property rights to the benefit of the creditor. Something which the Freezing Order cannot achieve being limited to an *in personam* remedy enforceable only against the debtor and not the assets themselves. But the French *Saisie Conservatoire* is limited to assets located in France unlike the World Wide Freezing Order. Last but not least, unlike England, France does not appear to have maintained its influence in the legal sphere in Francophone jurisdictions. By way of example, the recent reform of the French Civil Code for the first time since it was drafted in the early nineteenth century was promoted vigorously by the French lawyers. However, it has attracted little interest from outside of France though many former French colonies in North and West Africa have similar legal concepts to *the Saisie Conservatoire* in force.

The United States obviously is a major jurisdiction but surprisingly conservative in comparison to its former common law ancestor the United Kingdom. Paradoxically the Mareva Injunction could have been adopted by the US Federal Courts but their Supreme Court in the famous *Grupo Mexicano* case decided that this was an issue reserved for Congress. And there is little evidence that the American legal system has much influence in English speaking countries outside of the United States in terms of adoption of American legal concepts unlike England.

In the case of Hungary the conclusion which is difficult to avoid is that here is clearly a legal vacuum in relation to provisional measures. Hungary is a civil law country so it is unlikely that the courts will be able to follow the example of the English judges in creating new remedies. Legislation would therefore be required. That, however, would presume re-evaluation of the very foundations of the existing legal framework. This because Hungary now stands out not only as the legal system that lacks *ex parte* provisional measures but also as a jurisdiction in which this area of law has almost completely escaped the attention of both scholars and lawmakers. Hence, the pivotal questions of whether Hungarians would follow the Mareva model or be more tempted by the French civil law concepts? Or possibly in the alternative the EU would provide them with a pan European solution? These are questions which simply cannot be answered at the moment.

The EU is of course determined to facilitate cross-border enforcement of judgments. The recent European Account Preservation Orders (EAPOs) is a striking example of such an initiative. And the departure of one of the major EU jurisdictions—the United Kingdom—may influence the EU to take a more active role here to compete with an ex member it would be tempted to isolate. The main problem with EU initiatives, however, is that they are often emasculated, if not effectively side lined, by the Member States, reducing potential 'nuclear weapons to paper tigers.

Until the next major milestone in future legal developments is reached by either courts or lawmakers that would lead to essential principles being revisited and attracting renewed attention, comparative scholarship should be tempted to pick up the gauntlet and explore the hereinbefore largely bypassed topics that explain the efficiency the Mareva Injunction and other cutting edge provisional measures. As we have suggested earlier in this review, these should include analysis of the roles of contempt of court rules, the co-existence of supportive ancillary measures, the creation of inchoate liens and the extent of the discretion of the judges in deciding to award the measures may play.

In the light of all these factors, it seems that the Mareva Injunction, in the absence of any other viable initiatives from its competitors, will continue for the time being to rule the waves as the most effective provisional measure.

FSC
www.fsc.org
MIX
Papier | Fördert
gute Waldnutzung
FSC® C083411

Kolibri 360 GmbH
Ferdinand-Jühlke-Straße 7
99095 Erfurt, Deutschland
produktsicherheit@kolibri360.de